The New

D1210026

POCKET
**MBA**
SERIES

# TRACKING & CONTROLLING COSTS
## 25 KEYS TO COST MANAGEMENT

MOHAMED HUSSEIN, PH.D.
**University of Connecticut**

**Lebhar-Friedman Books**
NEW YORK • CHICAGO • LOS ANGELES • LONDON • PARIS • TOKYO

For *The New York Times*
Mike Levitas, Editorial Director, Book Development
Tom Redburn, General Series Editor
Brent Bowers, Series Editor
James Schembari, Series Editor

Lebhar-Friedman Books
425 Park Avenue
New York, NY 10022

Published by Lebhar-Friedman Books
Lebhar-Friedman Books is a company of Lebhar-Friedman Inc.

Printed in the United States of America

**Library of Congress Cataloging-in-Publication Data**
Hussein, Mohamed ElMutassim.
      Tracking & controlling costs : 25 keys to cost management /
Mohamed Hussein.
      p.   cm.—(The New York Times pocket MBA series ; vol. 7)
      Includes index.
      ISBN 0-86730-777-3 (pbk.)
      1. Financial statements.   2. Cost accounting.   3. Cash flow.
I. Title.   II. Title: Tracking & controlling a costs.   III. Series.
      HF5681.B2 H84   1999
      658.15'52—dc21                                99-27689
                                                              CIP

DESIGN & PRODUCTION BY MILLER WILLIAMS DESIGN ASSOCIATES

Visit our Web site at lfbooks.com

## INTRODUCTION

**LEBHAR-FRIEDMAN BOOKS** is proud to present *The New York Times* Pocket MBA Series, 12 invaluable reference volumes that are easily accessible to all businesspersons, from first level managers to the executive suite. The books are written by Ph.D.s who teach in the MBA programs in some of the finest schools in the country. A team of business editors from *The New York Times*—Mike Levitas, Tom Redburn, Brent Bowers, and James Schembari—provided their own expertise to edit a reference series that is beyond compare.

*The New York Times* Pocket MBA Series offers quick-reference key points learned in top MBA programs. The 25-key structure of each volume presents an unparalleled synopsis of crucial principles of specific areas of business expertise. The unique approach to this series packages academic books for consumers in an easy-to-use trade format that is ideal for the individual businessperson as well as an excellent training reference manual. Be sure to get all 12 titles in the series to complete your own MBA education.

Joseph Mills
Senior Managing Editor
Lebhar-Friedman Books

*The New York Times* Pocket MBA
Series includes these 12 volumes:

**Analyzing Financial Statements**

**Business Planning**

**Business Financing**

**Growing & Managing a Business**

**Organizing a Company**

**Forecasting Budgets**

**Tracking & Controlling Costs**

**Sales & Marketing**

**Managing Investment**

**Going Global**

**Leadership & Vision**

**The Board of Directors**

# 25 KEYS TO COST MANAGEMENT

## CONTENTS

# KEY 1

## *Strategic cost management*

There are three main business objectives: make profits, beat the competition, and satisfy customers. It sounds simple, but to achieve the first two you must accomplish the third. Through a sophisticated understanding of the cost structure of the firm, information about those costs is used to develop strategies to produce the highest possible quality at the lowest cost, and, hence, gain a competitive advantage.

According to Shank and Govindarajan (1993), strategic cost management blends three themes: 1) Strategic positioning where a business competes either by having lower costs (cost leadership), or superior products (product differentiation); 2) Value chain analysis, which encompasses both an external focus (supply chain cost analysis and customer chain cost analysis) and an internal focus that extends beyond the manufacturing to include product development at one end and marketing at the other end. I'll get more into these later. 3) Cost drivers that go beyond the traditional thinking of assuming that the amount of output is the driver of costs.

## STRATEGIC POSITIONING

Firms following each of the two strategies would require different types of costing systems because their focus is different. A cost leader needs to maintain tight control over its costs and continually find ways to reduce them. On the other hand, a product differentiator would require a system that enables it to monitor the frequency and speed of introducing new products and also the efficiency of the product development process, product cycle costs, and marketing costs. It is important to note that a low-cost producer still has to maintain a minimum level of quality if it is to compete. Low cost does not mean cheap products. Customers demand value. On the other hand, customers will not buy inferior products at any price.

A firm that adopts a cost leadership strategy seeks to become the lowest-cost producer in its industry. The cost leader can set prices that enable it to take full advantage of its cost efficiencies. The critical advantage of a cost leadership strategy is that the leader can threaten competitors with a price war if they do not behave.

A cost leader requires information necessary to control as well as lower costs of products and/or processes. Activity-based costing systems are used to identify cost drivers and measure costs accurately. Operating budgets and continuous improvement techniques are used to control and reduce costs. Continuous improvement becomes a way of life. To lower its costs and avoid a price increase, Toyota redesigned the Camry to reduce its number of components and was able to offer it at the prior year price. Shank and Govindarajan (1993) recommend that a cost leader should emphasize the importance of meeting budgets, the role of product cost as an input to pricing decisions, and the importance of competitors' cost analysis.

A firm following a differentiation strategy seeks to make customers perceive that its products are superior to its competitors' and willingly pay prices high enough to offset the cost of differentiation. Cooper (1994) noted that a sustainable competitive advantage of a differentiating strategy requires barriers to imitation, which is not always possible in the current competitive environment. The president of Codman & Shertleff, a subsidiary of Johnson & Johnson that specializes in surgical implements, lamented (Simon, 1987):

> "In the past, we concentrated on producing superior quality goods, and the market was willing to pay whatever it took to get the best. But the environment has changed; the shift has been massive. We are trying to adapt to a situation where doctors and hospitals are under severe pressure to be more efficient and cost-effective."

Reverse engineering and the fast reaction of lean enterprises to competitors' new products make competitive advantage temporary. To defend its position, a differentiating firm is forced to introduce new products quickly. But customers may not be ready to replace their equipment and they may not be willing to pay a premium. A good example is Intel's Pentium processor. The period between generations of chips is getting shorter; Intel is having a difficult time convincing the market of the need for the enhanced capabilities of its new chips and has to settle for lower prices (*Business Week*, March 22, 1999).

To meet the challenges of smaller volumes and lower prices, these firms need information to balance the need for R&D and control of R&D costs.

## THE VALUE CHAIN

Porter (1985) coined the term the value chain to describe the set of value-creating activities from the extraction of raw materials to delivery of the final product to the customer. So the value chain extends beyond the boundaries of the firm to encompass its suppliers and distributors. For a firm to be competitive, it must have an efficient value chain. The recent success of Chrysler can be attributed to its ability to increase the efficiency of its internal and external value chains. The result is a decrease in the cost of developing a new model by 40 percent and a reduction in the time it takes to bring a new model to market from 234 weeks to 160 weeks (Dyer, 1996). The external components of the value chain will be discussed in Key 19.

The internal value chain extends from research and development to customer support (see chart). In the past, firms concentrated on controlling production cost because it represented the largest portion of its total cost. However, shorter product life cycles, product variety and demanding customers have increased the proportion of the costs of activities upstream and downstream from production.

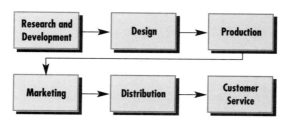

For example, the shorter life cycle means that development costs have to be recovered over a smaller volume and results in a higher development cost per unit. The increase in extended warranties and channels of distribution (e.g., discount clubs such as Sam's Club, discount outlets, specialty stores and mail-order retailers) have increased the marketing costs. For example, in a case about the Swedish firm Kanthal, Kaplan (1989) reported that its marketing expenses equal 34 percent of its total costs, while its manufacturing labor represented only 19 percent. A firm cannot afford to neglect the control of 34 percent of its costs! More importantly, Kanthal found that the 5 percent most profitable customers provided 150 percent of its profits and the 10 percent least profitable customers lost 120 percent of the profits. Controlling marketing and customer support costs is critical to profitability.

## STRATEGIC COST DRIVERS

Traditional cost systems assume that costs are driven primarily by volume: the more you produce, the higher your costs. Volume drivers such as units of output, labor hours or machine hours are used to allocate indirect cost to products and services. This assumption is no longer valid. In modern complex firms that produce and sell a variety of products or services, there are many factors that drive costs. In many cases the relationship between costs and costs drivers may not be apparent, and in most cases the cost drivers are the result of long-term decisions. Shank and Govindarajan (1993) classify strategic cost drivers into two groups: structural and executional cost drivers. There are five structural cost drivers:

1. Scale is the size of investment in research and development, manufacturing, and marketing resources.

2. Scope is the level of vertical integration, which is when a firm performs activities required for the production of a product internally rather than outsourcing.

**3** Experience is the number of times the firm has done the activity.

**4** Technology is the process technologies used in each step in the firm's value chain.

**5** Complexity is the variety of products or services offered by the firm.

The executional drivers include:

- ◆ Work force involvement in continuous improvement.
- ◆ Total quality management.
- ◆ Capacity utilization, given the scale investment.
- ◆ Plant layout efficiency.
- ◆ Product configuration. Is the design or formulation effective?
- ◆ Exploiting linkages with suppliers and customers.

Managing these cost drivers requires strategic long-term decisions. Shank and Govindarajan note that cost control would require minimizing structural drivers and maximizing executional drivers.

Traditional cost management systems are not capable of providing business managers with information necessary to manage efficiently in the current globally competitive environment. Strategic cost management that integrates strategic positioning, value chain analysis and strategic cost drivers is what is needed.

# KEY 2

## *Understanding costs and cost behavior*

A cost is simply the sacrifice or commitment of resources of an organization in exchange for a current or future benefit. Proper classification of costs is important for measuring, analyzing, communicating and controlling those costs. Costs can be classified in several different ways. Before we can classify costs, we have to identify the object whose cost we are classifying. The following are definitions of cost terms that help cost classification, measurement, communication and control:

Cost object: An item or activity for which separate cost measurement is desired (e.g. products, services, activities, departments, customers).

Cost is the monetary value of goods and services expended to obtain current or future benefits.

Capitalized costs are plant, equipment, trucks; expensed costs are cost of goods sold, marketing expenses, etc.

Expenses are either costs for which benefits expired in the current period (such as cost of goods sold), or costs whose benefits cannot be matched easily with the products or services of another period (such as advertising).

Cost driver: Any factor that affects costs. A change in the cost driver will cause a change in the total cost of a related cost object. Examples of cost drivers include units produced, labor hours, invoices processed.

Direct cost: Cost that can be traced to a specific cost object.

Indirect cost: Cost that cannot be traced to a specific cost object. Examples of indirect costs are utilities, repairs and maintenance. These costs are allocated to cost objects using cost-allocation methods. These are explained in Key 4.

### Costs in Manufacturing Organizations

Product costs are associated with manufacturing and include direct material costs, direct labor cost, and manufacturing overhead.

$$\text{Direct materials} + \text{Direct labor} = \text{Prime costs}$$

$$\text{Direct labor} + \text{Manufacturing overhead} = \text{Conversion costs}$$

Period costs are costs treated as expenses in the period in which they are incurred because they cannot be associated with the manufacture of products. Selling and administrative expenses are period costs.

Production volume is the measure, such as number of units, of various products manufactured in a time period.

In traditional cost systems, direct labor is treated as a prime cost and considered to be the main driver of manufacturing overhead costs. This was the case before automation. Automation and product variety contributed to the decrease of labor as a percentage of total production cost and the increase in the percentage of overhead. In most modern factories, direct labor does not represent more than 5 percent of total manufacturing costs. Hence, more attention is being paid to manufacturing overhead. Activity-based costing systems (ABC) are developed to accurately attribute overhead to products and services. The following classifications are used in ABC systems:

Unit-related activities are tied to the number of units produced. Examples of costs are direct materials, direct labor, and energy.

Batch-related activities are those related to the number of batches. (When products are produced more than one unit at a time, the group of units is called a batch.) Examples are machine set-up and first unit testing.

Product-sustaining activities are those performed to support the production of products. Examples are product specifications and engineering changes.

Facility-sustaining activities are those performed to manage the upkeep of the plant. Examples are supervisory costs, maintenance, janitorial services and property taxes.

### COSTS IN SERVICE ORGANIZATIONS
Services produced cannot be inventoried for future sale, thus, cost accounting systems associated with most service organizations do not have to worry about inventory valuation.

# Nothing stings more deeply than the loss of money.

*Livy*, **History**

Output is difficult to measure as services produce less tangible and measurable products than manufacturing organizations.

Operating overhead is the indirect costs of producing services in a service organization.

### COST BEHAVIOR
Costs are classified based on how they respond to changes in the activities being costed. Costs that increase proportionate to the activity are classified as variable costs. Costs that do not change when the activity changes are classified as fixed costs. Costs that are neither totally variable nor fixed are classified as mixed costs or semi-variable costs. These four categories of costs are described below using graphs.

Variable cost: Cost that changes proportionally to changes of a cost driver (see graph).

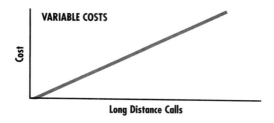

Example: Your total long distance telephone bill is based on how many minutes you talk.

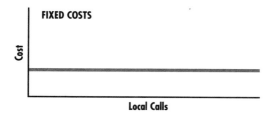

Fixed cost: Cost that does not change despite changes of a cost driver (see graph). Example: Your monthly basic telephone bill probably does not change when you make more local calls.

Mixed cost: Cost that is comprised of both fixed and variable cost components (see graph). Your electric bill usually has a fixed charge for the service and a variable charge based on consumption.

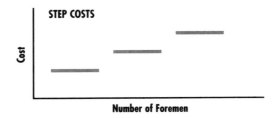

**STEP COSTS**

Cost

**Number of Foremen**

Step cost: Costs that increase in steps. For example, increasing the cost of supervision by hiring a new foreman every time the number of employees exceeds that which can be supervised by the current foremen (see graph).

Average (unit) cost: Total cost divided by some volume measure. Average cost must be used within relevant range.

| Behavior of Total Costs and Unit Costs When Changes Occur in the Level of the Cost Driver | | |
|---|---|---|
| | **Total Costs** | **Unit Costs** |
| Variable costs | Change | Remain the same |
| Fixed costs | Remain the same | Change |

# KEY 3

## Costing systems

An important function of a cost system is the accumulation of costs of products and services including the costs of sales. The following chart depicts the cost flow process:

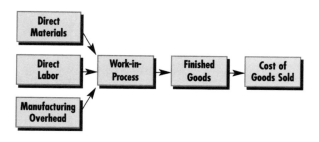

A cost system has to fit the nature of products/services and operations of an organization. Two prototypes are used to describe organizations. One is a job-order organization where each job has some unique features. The second is a process type organization where each product or service has homogeneous units. Two costing systems are proposed to fit these two types of organizations: job costing system that traces costs to individual units or to specific jobs, contracts, or batches of goods; process costing system used when identical units are produced through a series of uniform production steps.

**Job Order Organization Examples:**

| Service | Merchandising | Manufacturing |
|---|---|---|
| Engineering firm | Furniture Retailer | Aircraft parts |
| Auto repair shop | CD distributor | Machine shop |

**Process Type Organization Examples:**

| Service | Merchandising | Manufacturing |
|---|---|---|
| Banking | Food wholesaler | Oil refining |
| Telephone service | Magazine subscription | Food processor |

### GENERAL APPROACH TO JOB COSTING

Products are produced as individual jobs to meet unique specifications. Much of the manufacturing costs are easily traced to specific products. A cost sheet is used to accumulate the materials, labor and manufacturing overhead costs of each job.

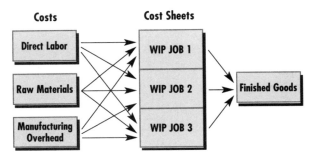

### APPLYING MANUFACTURING OVERHEAD TO PRODUCTS

Jobs are usually charged for the actual costs of direct materials and direct labor. Manufacturing overhead costs are charged to jobs based on estimates. There are two reasons estimates are used. 1) To save the clerical cost of determining how much of the actual cost of each item should be charged to each job. 2) Some of the overhead costs, such as preventive maintenance, are incurred at one point in time but benefit jobs worked on during the whole year. The following five steps are used to apply manufacturing overhead to jobs:

**1** Choose a cost allocation base (e.g., direct labor hours, direct labor costs, or machine hours).

**2** Prepare factory overhead budget with budgeted total overhead and budgeted total volume of application base.

**3** Compute budgeted factory overhead rate:

> Budgeted factory overhead cost rate =
> Budgeted total factory overhead cost ÷
> Budgeted total quantity of allocation base

**4** Apply overhead to jobs based on the actual application base.

**5** At year-end, account for difference between actual and applied manufacturing overhead. Use the information about the difference to adjust the costs of products and improve estimate of future manufacturing overhead rate.

#### GENERAL APPROACH TO PROCESS COSTING

In a process costing system, costs are accumulated in a department or process using a cost of production report. Costs are averaged over all units processed during a period. Five steps are used in preparing a cost of production report. Because some units may be incomplete at the end of the operating period, we measure their level of completion and translate it into equivalent complete units.

**Cost is the father and compensation is the mother of progress.**

*J.G. Holland,* **Plain Talks**

## FIVE STEPS IN PROCESS COSTING

**1** Summarize flow of physical units using the following equation:

Beginning work in progress (W.I.P.) + Units started = Units completed + Ending work in progress

**2** Create a common measure of completed and incomplete units by estimating the equivalent complete units in the work done in the incomplete units.

**3** Summarize total costs for W.I.P.

**4** Compute equivalent unit costs. Divide total costs (from Step 3) by equivalent units (from Step 2) for both direct materials and conversion costs.

**5** Apply costs to completed units and ending W.I.P.

The equivalent unit costs (direct materials and conversion costs) are now applied to the finished goods and the ending W.I.P.

| Cost of Production Report | (1) Physical Flow | (2) Equivalent units | |
|---|---|---|---|
| | | Materials | Conversion |
| Units to be accounted for: | | | |
| Beg. W.I.P | 2,000 | | |
| Started | 38,000 | | |
| Total to account for | 40,000 | | |
| | | | |
| Units accounted for: | | | |
| Completed & transferred | 36,000 | 36,000 | 36,000 |
| Ending W.I.P. | 4,000 | 4,000 | 1,000 |
| Total units accounted for | 40,000 | 40,000 | 37,000 |
| (3) Costs to acct. for: | Total | Materials | Conversion |
| Beg. W.I.P. | $5,364 | $1,760 | $3,604 |
| Current | $111,336 | $37,240 | $74,096 |
| Total costs (a) | $116,700 | $39,000 | $77,700 |
| Equivalent units (b) | | 40,000 | 37,000 |
| (4) Unit cost a÷b | | $0.975 | $2.10 |
| | | | |
| **(5) Costs applied as follows:** | | | |
| To units completed and transferred 36,000 × ($.975 + $2.10) = $110,700 | | | |
| To ending W.I.P.: | | | |
| Materials | 4,000 × $.975 = | $3,900 | |
| Conversion | 1,000 × $2.10 = | $2,100 | $6,000 |
| Total cost applied | | | $116,700 |

## HYBRID SYSTEMS

Many firms combine the features of both job and process systems. A shoemaker may use a batch system where one batch may be sneakers and the next dress shoes. Each batch will be costed as a job and the units within it will be charged at the average cost per unit in the batch.

# KEY 4

## *Assigning indirect costs*

**D**irect labor and direct materials can be traced to products and are called direct costs. Overhead costs can not be easily traced to a product. These costs are indirect costs and must be allocated to the products. Indirect costs are still product costs and must be attached to units produced.

Cost allocation involves the assignment of indirect costs (e.g., manufacturing overhead) to different departments or products. There is no best way to do this, but we try to find a reasonable allocation method with the goal of minimizing cost distortions and perhaps improving overall firm performance through efficient utilization of common resources.

### PURPOSES OF COST ALLOCATION
  ◆ To make economic decisions for resource allocation.
  ◆ To motivate managers and employees.
  ◆ To justify costs or compute reimbursements.

◆ To measure income and assets for reporting to external users such as customers, creditors and investors.

#### CRITERIA TO GUIDE COST ALLOCATION DECISIONS

The activity that causes the consumption of the resources should be used to allocate the cost to cost objects. For example, consumption of supplies might be caused by the operation of machines, in which case machine hours can be used as the allocation base. This is the favored criterion, however the consumption of many overhead items may not be tied to a specific activity. Then, one of the following three criteria may be used:

◆ Benefits received—where the benefits received by different products, services or departments from the consumption of the resources can be measured.
◆ Fairness or equity—a method that can be perceived as fair by the different departments.
◆ Ability to bear—(e.g., using sales revenues as a base of allocation).

#### STEPS IN COST ALLOCATION

**1** The first step in cost allocation is to create cost pools. One criterion for selecting an indirect cost pool is homogeneity (i.e., each activity in the pool has the same cause-and-effect relationship between the cost driver and the activity cost). Examples of cost pools are cost of purchasing department, cost of indirect production labor, and cost of equipment maintenance.

**2** The second step is to select a cost allocation base for each indirect cost pool.

**3** The third step it to establish rate per unit of cost allocation base.

### EXAMPLE OF MANUFACTURING OVERHEAD COST ALLOCATION:

A firm produces two products, X and Q. The firm uses direct labor hours to allocate manufacturing overhead. It has $100,000 budgeted manufacturing overhead and an estimated 10,000 direct labor hours (D.L.H.). Actual output of product X required 6,000 D.L.H. and product Q required 4,000 D.L.H.

First, compute overhead rate:

$$\text{Overhead rate} = \frac{\$100,000}{10,000 \text{ D.L.H.}} = \$10 \text{ per D.L.H.}$$

Second, allocate overhead as follows:

Product X will be charged with $10 × 6,000 = $60,000
Product Q will be charged with $10 × 4,000 = $40,000

### SUPPORT UNITS COSTS ALLOCATION

In almost all firms there are two types of units. Producing units that are engaged in producing the products or services sold by the firm to its customers, and support units (e.g., personnel department, maintenance department, etc.) that provide services to other units within the firm. Before the costs of the support departments can be charged to the products or services they have to flow into the producing departments.

There are three methods for allocating the costs of support departments: direct allocation, which ignores services provided by support departments to each other; a reciprocal method that allocates a support unit's cost to both the support and producing units it serves, which entails recognizing reciprocal services, and a step-down method that allows partial allocations across support departments. The following example illustrates the three methods.

The Inco Corporation has two production departments, smelting (SM) and extrusion (EX), and two major service departments, material handling (M.H.) and power generation (P.G.). The costs and outputs of the service departments are given below:

|  | M.H. | P.G. | SM | EX |
|---|---|---|---|---|
| Traceable costs | $10,000 | $4,000 | — | — |
| Tons moved | — | 20 | 50 | 30 |
| Power used, kWh | 50 | — | 40 | 10 |

Direct allocation method: Ignoring service department interactions, costs are directly allocated to producing departments:

| | |
|---|---|
| SM: (5/8) $10,000 + (4/5) $4,000 = | $9,450 |
| EX: (3/8) $10,000 + (1/5) $4,000 = | $4,550 |
| Total costs allocated: | $14,000 |

Step-down method: Since 50 percent of P.G.'s output goes to M.H., we will allocate P.G.'s costs first.

|  | M.H. | P.G. | SM | EX |
|---|---|---|---|---|
| Traceable costs | $10,000 | $4,000 | — | — |
| PG | $2,000 | ($4,000) | $1,600 | $400 |
| MH | ($12,000) | | $7,500 | $4,500 |
| Reallocated costs | 0 | 0 | $9,100 | $4,900 |

Reciprocal method: Let Xm and Xp be the reallocated costs of service departments, M.H. and P.G., respectively. Solving the simultaneous equations:

$$Xm = \$10,000 + 0.5\ Xp$$
$$Xp = \$4000 + 0.2\ Xm$$

yields:
$$Xm = \$13,333$$
$$Xp = \$6,667$$

Note also that $Xm + Xp = \$13,333 + \$6,667 = \$20,000 > \$14,000$.

Allocated costs to producing departments:

SM: (0.5) $13,333 + (0.4) $6,667 = $9,333
EX: (0.3) $13,333 + (0.1) $6,667 = $4,667
Total costs allocated:      $14,000

## CONSEQUENCES OF INAPPROPRIATE COST ALLOCATION BASES

For example, if direct labor cost is used as an allocation base, the following results may appear:

- ◆ Excessive use of external suppliers for parts with high direct labor.
- ◆ Too much concern over direct labor hours at the expense of materials or machining costs.
- ◆ Attempt to classify production labor as indirect labor.
- ◆ Under- or over-costing of products or services.

## COST ALLOCATION: JOINT PRODUCTS

Many industries have joint products where you cannot produce one product without the others. An oil refinery cannot produce gasoline without also producing fuel oil and heavy distillates. Such industries have to allocate the joint costs up to the split-off point between the joint products.

## METHODS FOR ALLOCATING JOINT COSTS

There are four methods to allocate joint costs to joint products. We will use a simple example to illustrate those methods. Suppose a joint process results in two products: Product X and Product Y. In one period, 30 pounds of X and 20 pounds of Y were produced at a total joint cost of $20.

**Make money and the whole nation will conspire to call you a gentlemen.**

*Robert C. Edwards,* **Summer Annual**

Sales Value at Split-off point method:

|  | Product X | Product Y |
|---|---|---|
| Sales value | $10 | $40 |
| Weighting | 0.2 | 0.8 |
| Joint costs allocation | $4 | $16 |

Estimated Net Realizable Value (N.R.V.) method:

|  | Product X | Product Y |
|---|---|---|
| Expected final sales value | $40 | $60 |
| Less separable costs | ($15) | ($35) |
| Estimated N.R.V. at split-off | $25 | $25 |
| Weighting | 0.5 | 0.5 |
| Joint costs allocation | $10 | $10 |

Constant Gross-Margin Percentage N.R.V. method:

Step 1: Compute overall gross-margin percentage

| | |
|---|---|
| Expected final sales value | $100 |
| Less joint & separable costs | ($70*) |
| Gross margin | $30 |
| Gross margin percentage | 30% |
| Joint costs ($20) plus separable costs ($50) | |

Steps 2 & 3:

| | Product X | Product Y |
|---|---|---|
| Expected final sales value | $40 | $60 |
| Less gross margin (30 percent) | ($12) | ($18) |
| Cost of goods sold | $28 | $42 |
| Less separable costs | ($15) | ($35) |
| Joint costs allocated | $13 | $7 |

Physical Measure method:

| | Product X | Product Y |
|---|---|---|
| Physical measure in pounds | 30 pounds | 20 pounds |
| Weighting | 0.6 | 0.4 |
| Joint costs allocation | $12 | $8 |

## No allocation of joint costs

Some firms do not allocate joint costs because of the lack of cause-and-effect relationships. Inventories are carried at estimated net realizable values less a normal profit margin. Examples of some industries include mining, oil refining, and food processing.

## Irrelevance of joint costs for decision making

Joint costs are irrelevant in decision making because changing the method of allocation can change the amount of cost allocated to a product. The only costs relevant in decision making are costs that are different between alternatives. For example, the decision to sell a joint product at the point of split-off or process further should be based on the difference between the incremental revenue and the incremental cost.

# KEY 5

## *Activity-based costing*

The following changes have made the traditional costing system inappropriate for many firms:

- Intensified global competition and new technologies have made accurate cost information crucial to competitive success.
- Product lines and marketing channels have proliferated.
- Factory support operations, marketing, distribution, and engineering costs have exploded.
- Direct labor is a small fraction of product costs.
- Many cost categories do not vary with short-term changes in output, but do vary with changes over a period of years in design, mix and range of products and customers.
- Ninety percent of costs are determined in the design phase.

# Taking it all in all, I find it more trouble to watch after money than to get it.

**Montaigne**

The traditional system is being replaced by activity-based costing systems that have the following characteristics:

- Focus on expensive resources.
- Emphasize resources whose consumption varies by product.
- Focus on resources whose use is not correlated with traditional allocation bases such as direct labor.
- Identify drivers of costs (e.g., the bulk of any factory overhead costs are associated with ordering parts, keeping track of them, inspecting them and setting up to produce components).
- Use cost drivers to influence behavior, especially for product designers.

Base product cost on the measurement of:

- What creates work and the quantity of work demanded by each product.
- Approximate the long-run demands on resources by each product.
- Product costs should include more than material, labor and overhead.
- Costs such as engineering design, servicing and marketing should be included.
- Expenses that benefit future products (e.g., basic research and idle capacity should not be included).

### ACTIVITIES

An activity is any event or transaction that is a cost driver. Examples of such activities include:

| | |
|---|---|
| Machine setups | Maintenance requests |
| Purchase orders | Machine time |
| Quality inspections | Power consumed |
| Production orders | Beds occupied |
| Blood tests | Flight-hours logged |

Activity-based costing improves costing systems in four ways:

**1** It increases the number of cost pools used to accumulate overhead costs. Rather than accumulate all overhead costs in a single, company-wide pool (or in departments), costs are accumulated by activity. For example, set-up costs, material handling and engineering changes are accumulated in separate pools.

**2** It changes the bases used to assign overhead cost to products. Rather than assigning costs on the basis of a measure of volume (such as direct labor-hours or machine-hours), costs are assigned based on the activities that generate the costs.

**3** It changes the nature of many overhead costs. Costs that were formerly indirect (depreciation, power, inspection) are traced to specific activities thus eliminating the need for allocation.

**4** It is easy to backtrack through the A.B.C. system to discover where in the organization the resource consumption occurs that has been attributed to products, customers, etc.

### Costs hierarchy

Many of the resources consumed by a product do not vary with how much is produced. Some resources are consumed by the number of production runs, the length of the setups required to make the product, and how many times units under production are moved. Other resources are consumed just to have the ability to produce the product, or to keep the factory open and operating throughout the year. They do not increase if volume increases nor will they decrease if volume decreases.

A hierarchical model divides costs into four categories: facility sustaining, product sustaining, batch and unit level (Cooper and Kaplan, 1991). Facility sustaining costs are those of the activities necessary to maintain a factory in a working condition. Examples are supervisory personnel, janitorial services and building maintenance.

Product sustaining costs are those of activities necessary to develop and process a product. Examples include product specifications, engineering change and process engineering.

Batch costs are those of activities performed every time a batch is processed. Examples are costs of machine set-up, material movement and inspection.

Unit level costs are those of the units manufactured. They include materials, labor and energy.

## COMPARISON OF TRADITIONAL AND A.B.C. SYSTEMS

The Ro Corporation makes minivans and sedans. For many years the firm has used a manufacturing overhead rate based on direct labor hours. A new controller has suggested that an activity-based costing system may improve the accuracy of product costs. She explained that by creating an overhead rate for each production activity that causes overhead costs, the resulting product costs will reflect an accurate measure of overhead cost.

The manufacturing overhead rate for April 1992 using the traditional overhead allocation scheme is $25 per direct labor hour. After studying the plant's production activities and costs, the controller provides the following activities and activity-based overhead rates:

|  | Products | |
|---|---|---|
|  | Minivans | Sedans |
| Quantity produced | 50 | 100 |
| D.L.H. used | 100 | 300 |
| Direct labor cost | $1,000 | $3,000 |
| Number of times handled | 40 | 20 |
| Number of parts | 10 | 6 |
| Number of design changes | 5 | 3 |
| Number of setups | 7 | 5 |

The activity-based overhead rates are as follows:

| Handling | $50 per handling |
|---|---|
| Number of parts | $100 per part |
| Design changes | $375 per change |
| Setups | $200 per setup |

Total direct materials costs were $4,250 and $7,500 for minivans and sedans, respectively.

The cost using the traditional overhead allocation method:

|  | Minivans | Sedans |
|---|---|---|
| Direct materials costs | $4,250 | $7,500 |
| Direct labor | 1,000 | 3,000 |
| Overhead @$25 per labor hour | 2,500 | 7,500 |
| Total | 7,750 | 18,000 |

The cost using the A.B.C. overhead allocation method:

|  | Minivans | | Sedans | |
|---|---|---|---|---|
| Direct materials costs | | $4,250 | | $7,500 |
| Direct labor | | 1,000 | | 3,000 |
| Overhead: | | | | |
| Handling | $50 × 40 | 2,000 | $50 × 20 | 1,000 |
| No. of parts | 100 × 10 | 1,000 | 100 × 6 | 600 |
| Design changes | 375 × 5 | 1,875 | 375 × 3 | 1,125 |
| Setups | 200 × 7 | 1,400 | 200 × 5 | 1,000 |
| Total overhead | | 6,275 | | 3,725 |
| Total | | $11,525 | | $14,225 |

Although the total costs have not changed, the cost of each of the two products has changed when the method of allocation is changed from the traditional to the A.B.C. If we accept that the A.B.C. method more accurately reflects the consumption of resources, then the sedans were subsidizing the minivans under the traditional method. This information should help the firm set the prices of the two products more accurately and develop a strategy for product promotion.

# KEY 6

## *Just-in-time production system*

A just-in-time (J.I.T.) production system obtains materials just in time for production and provides finished goods just in time for sale. The objective of this system is to reduce inventory levels. This is accomplished by producing small numbers of units at a time, using high quality materials and components, and having strong long-term relationships with suppliers and a flexible work force. J.I.T. is more than a mere inventory control system. It also tries to:

◆ Remove non-value-added activities (e.g., inventory, storage, and handling)
◆ Simplify and streamline operations
◆ Minimize overall company costs
◆ Improve product quality through Total Quality Control (T.Q.C.)
◆ Increase productivity

**MAJOR FEATURES OF J.I.T.**
◆ Eliminates inventory

- Stops production if parts are missing or defective
- Reduces production cycle time
- Simplifies production activities

### REQUIREMENTS FOR J.I.T. AND T.Q.C.
- Employee involvement through work-related (Quality Circles)
- Social (team sports)
- Good relationship with vendors

### BENEFITS OF J.I.T.
- Reduces investment in inventories
- Reduces inventory costs by purchasing materials immediately preceding use

J.I.T. reduces the costs of inventory ordering through:

- Reduced number of suppliers
- Long-term supplier contracts
- Reduced receiving inspection
- Reduced number of payments to suppliers
- Reduced risk of obsolescence
- Reduced need for factory space
- Reduced total manufacturing costs

The risk is that low inventory levels makes a company vulnerable if a supplier goes on strike or is unreliable in terms of timeliness of deliveries or quality of product. J.I.T. also puts pressure on marketing to provide the orders to keep the factory operating.

# KEY 7

## Inventory control

**M**ost organizations are not capable of meeting the ideal of a J.I.T. system because of fluctuations in demand and uncertainty in delivery by suppliers. Hence, inventories are needed to meet fluctuations in demand and supply. The optimal level of inventory is a function of the costs of lost sales due to running out of stock, the costs of holding inventories, and the costs of placing orders. The objective of inventory management is to reduce the costs of ordering and holding inventories.

That's where the economic order quantity equation comes in. The equation is used to identify the optimal order size that reduces total costs. The timing of the optimum order size is important. The reorder point is a function of the average daily demand, the lead-time, and the extra quantity kept to safeguard against turning customers away due to running out of stock

### THE REASONS FOR MAINTAINING INVENTORIES
There might be the need to fill orders quickly.

Customers may not be willing to wait and could opt to buy from competitors. Worse yet, their business may be lost for good.

Demand may be uncertain and difficult to forecast accurately. Inventories are needed to meet these fluctuations.

Even if suppliers are reliable there are important reasons to maintain inventories, such as maintaining a safety stock for unexpected events that require additional materials (e.g., rush orders), or to benefit from discounts for specific lot sizes that suppliers may offer. To take advantage of this kind of discount it may be necessary to order more than is currently needed, so the additional costs of holding the inventory should also be considered.

## MATERIAL REQUIREMENTS PLANNING (M.R.P.) SYSTEMS

◆ Based on finished goods required, planned production works backward to determine the raw materials needed. Using bill of material (B.O.M.), which lists all materials needed to produce a single unit of finished product, total materials needed = number of finished units times B.O.M. per unit (Example: The B.O.M. for a unit of Product A is 2 units of material X and 3 units of material Q. Total material needed to produce 5,000 units of product A equals 5,000 × 2 units of X + 5,000 × 3 units of Q.)

◆ M.R.P. is used when demand is known or predictable. M.R.P. can help reduce inventory levels significantly.

◆ When to order materials is a function of the production date and the lead-time on orders. Lead-time is the time necessary to place an order and receive the items.

◆ The order date is the production date minus the lead-time.

◆ When reliable suppliers are available, it is possible to reduce inventories to zero.

## THE DEVELOPMENT OF AN OPTIMAL INVENTORY LEVEL

The optimal level of inventories is a function of the costs of holding and the incremental cost of placing additional orders. Holding costs include the cost of capital invested in the inventory, warehousing costs, insurance and obsolescence. Ordering costs include the costs of selecting a supplier, placing an order, receiving, and processing an order.

## ELEMENTS IN THE TIMING OF INVENTORY PURCHASES

◆ The objective of inventory management is to reduce the costs of ordering and holding inventories. The costs of placing an order (C): These are the variable ordering costs. The costs to store a unit of inventory for a year (S): They include the variable costs connected with the average number of units in inventory and the cost of capital invested in inventory.

◆ The optimal order size, or economic order quantity (E.O.Q.), is the order size that will minimize the total ordering and holding costs. The following equation is used to calculate the E.O.Q.:

$$E.O.Q. = \frac{\sqrt{2AC}}{S}$$

Where:

$A$ = annual demand
$C$ = costs of placing an order
$S$ = costs of holding a unit for a year

◆ The timing of the optimum order size is also important. The reorder point is a function of the average daily demand, the lead-time, and the desired level of safety stock. Without safety stock, the reorder point (R.O.P.) is equal to the average daily demand multiplied by the lead-time in days.

R.O.P. = Average Daily Demand x Lead Time in Days

#### WAYS TO ESTIMATE THE SIZE OF SAFETY STOCK

- ◆ (Highest Daily demand − Average Demand) × Longest Lead Time, or
- ◆ Balance the cost of carrying the additional stock with the cost of running out of inventory.
- ◆ Meet stock-outs via back orders. The stock-out costs would consist of the cost to prepare a back order, the possible lost contribution margin on the sale, and the possible lost contribution on future sales.
- ◆ The cost of prediction errors in E.O.Q.— because the costs of holding inventory (S) and of placing an order (C) are so small in relation to the annual demand (A), errors in the estimates of these costs have little effect on the order quantity. This means these costs need only be reasonable and not absolutely accurate.

#### INVENTORY ACCOUNTING

Another factor in inventory control is the inventory accounting method. There are two of these: 1) Perpetual inventory method: Continuous recording of additions and withdrawals from the inventory accounts. 2) Periodic inventory method: Physical count needed at end of period to establish ending inventory. The perpetual method gives timely information on inventories, while the periodic is simple and less expensive.

# KEY 8

## *Quality as a cost driver*

The cost of poor quality can be a high percentage of total costs. Those costs can be classified into four categories of quality costs where trade-off can be made. Prevention costs are incurred to stop poor quality products from being produced, which include the costs of training, efficient design of products and processes. Appraisal costs incurred to identify poor products before shipment, which include quality inspection costs. Internal failure costs incurred because poor products exist and need to be corrected or replaced, which include the costs of rework. External failure costs are incurred to correct poor products that are delivered to customers. They include direct costs such as warranty costs as well as indirect costs such as losing future sales.

There are two competing views about the value of measuring and reporting the cost of quality (C.O.Q.). The proponents believe that reporting the cost of quality make people aware of the impact of poor quality on profits. C.O.Q. helps set priority for quality improvement. The cost of quality evaluates the performance of quality improvement. C.O.Q. determines optimal quality improvement alternatives. C.O.Q. focuses attention on major sources of quality costs.

The opponents of C.O.Q. argue that cost of quality measurement does not solve quality problems. C.O.Q. reports do not suggest specific actions. The cost of quality may not provide accurate short-term feedback. Effort and accomplishment may not match in a single time period. Important costs may be omitted from cost-of-quality reports and inappropriate costs may be included in those reports.

The opponents advocate using direct measures of quality (D.M.O.Q.) such as defect rates, machine up-time, the rate of production, adherence to production and delivery schedules, and the ratio of first quality units produced to total output. They see D.M.O.Q. as easily quantified and understood by factory employees. Direct measures of quality provide immediately useful information because they direct attention to a process that needs correction. However, D.M.O.Q. do not provide a single aggregate measure of quality performance.

### Costs of Quality
Prevention costs include inspection of materials upon delivery, inspection of production process, equipment inspection, and employee training,

Appraisal costs include finished goods inspection and field testing of products.

Internal failure costs are the cost of defects discovered before delivery to customers (e.g., scrap materials, rework, inspection of rework, lost sales resulting from late deliveries).

External failure costs are costs of defects discovered after delivery to customers. (e.g., warranty repairs, product liability, marketing costs to improve product image, lost sales due to poor product quality).

### USE OF COST OF QUALITY APPROACH IN ENVIRONMENTAL COSTS

Using the four C.O.Q. categories can help a firm reduce its environmental costs (Hughes and Willis, 1995). Prevention is the cost of insuring that products, processes and technologies are environmentally sound. It is an investment and should be done during the design phase of products, technologies and facilities. Prevention is the most cost effective. Appraisal costs are the costs of monitoring the firm's compliance with environmental requirements. Internal failure costs are the costs of correcting environmental problems by the firm. External failure costs are costs of enforcement and loss of goodwill. External failure costs are the highest because they can include punitive damages.

# KEY 9

## Cost-Volume-Profit relationships

According to the Institute of Management Accountants, "Profits depend upon a proper balance of selling prices, mix, volume, and costs." Cost-volume-profit (C.V.P.) analysis is one method used to analyze the impact of costs, prices and volume on profitability. It is popularly known as break-even analysis after the volume at which total revenues equal total costs. C.V.P. is based on the classification of cost behavior into variable and fixed. The contribution margin (C.M.) is the difference between revenue and variable cost and it is the amount left to cover fixed cost and provide profit. At the break-even volume, the contribution margin is equal to the fixed cost and profit is zero.

### BREAK-EVEN POINT

The break-even point is the point between making a profit or sustaining a loss. The break-even also lets a firm determine its margin of safety, which is the difference between its actual sales and its break-even sales volume (i.e., the amount by which sales have to fall before the firm will sustain a loss). The three methods for break-even analysis are the equation method, contribution-margin method, and graph method.

Equation method:

Sales − Variable costs − Fixed costs = Operating income

Set operating income = 0 to find the number of units at the break-even point

Contribution-margin method:

Break-even point in units =
Fixed costs / Unit contribution margin

Break-even point in dollars =
Fixed costs / Contribution margin ratio

Graph method:

The cost-volume-profit relationship can be presented graphically. The horizontal axis represents sales volume and the vertical axis is dollars of costs and revenue.

Example: Ms. Kerry Scott owns and operates the Java Joint, which sells regular coffee at $1.25 per cup, variable costs are $1.00 per cup and monthly fixed costs are $800. Determine the break-even in cups and in dollars.

Equation method:

Let $Q$ = number of cups
Break-even = $1.25Q − $1.00Q − $800 = 0
$.25Q = $800
$Q = $800 / $.25 = 3,200$ cups;
In dollars = 3,200 cups × $1.25 = $4,000

Contribution margin method:

$$\text{Contribution margin} = \$1.25 - \$1.00 = \$.25;$$
$$\text{CM ratio} = \$.25 / \$1.25 = .20$$
$$\text{Break-even} = \$800 / \$.25 = 3{,}200 \text{ cups}$$
$$\text{Break-even in dollar} = \$800 / .20 = \$4{,}000$$

Graphic method:

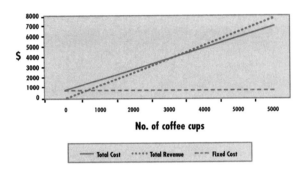

**No. of coffee cups**

— Total Cost   ····· Total Revenue   — — Fixed Cost

### TARGET OPERATING INCOME ANALYSIS

The C.V.P. method can be used to determine the sales volume necessary to achieve a certain profit. The analysis is similar to break-even analysis.

$$\text{Target volume} = \frac{\text{Fixed cost} + \text{Target profit}}{\text{Contribution margin}}$$

Example: Ms. Scott would like to make $600 in profit per month, how much sales does she needs to achieve her profit?

Assume no tax:

$$\text{Target volume} = \frac{\$800 + \$600}{\$.25} = 5{,}600 \text{ cups}$$

$$\text{Target revenue} = \frac{\$800 + \$600}{\$.20} = \$7{,}000$$

## Role of income taxes

$$\text{Target operating income} =$$
$$\text{Target net income} / [1 - \text{Tax rate}]$$

Assume 20 percent income tax:

$$\text{Target income before tax} = \frac{\$600}{(1-.20)} = \$750$$

$$\text{Target volume} = \frac{\$800 + \$750}{\$.25} = 6{,}200 \text{ cups}$$

$$\text{Target revenue} = \frac{\$800 + \$750}{\$.20} = \$7{,}750$$

## Effects of sales mix

Most firms have more than one product, and each product may have a different contribution to profits. In such cases the cost-volume-profit analysis is done using a weighted average contribution margin reflecting the sales mix.

Example: Assume that Ms. Scott has decided to add a second type of coffee, mocha, at $1.50 per cup and $1.20 variable cost. From a survey of her customers, she decided that her relative sale of regular coffee to mocha is 2:1. Monthly fixed costs are still $800.

Determine the monthly break-even sales volume in terms of cups of regular and mocha.

| | Regular | Mocha | Composite (2:1) |
|---|---|---|---|
| Selling price | $1.25 | $1.50 | $4.00 |
| Variable cost | $1.00 | $1.20 | $3.20 |
| Contribution margin | $0.25 | $0.30 | $0.80 |

Break-even volume of composite units = $800/$0.80 = 1,000 units

Therefore, break-even is 2,000 cups of regular coffee and 1,000 cups of mocha.

## ADVANTAGES AND DISADVANTAGES OF COST-VOLUME-PROFIT

Cost-volume-profit is a simple technique that can be used to communicate with people of different backgrounds and different levels of the organization. It provides information about volume, prices and costs, which should be of interest to everyone in the firm. It provides the information in numerical as well as graphical, form.

C.V.P. can be used to answer "what if" questions concerning changes in selling prices, variable costs, fixed costs or desired profit.

The disadvantages of the C.V.P. method are that it is a static analysis that has to be repeated every time one of the assumptions is changed. It also assumes prices and costs stay the same even with the change in volume.

# KEY 10

## *Customer profitability analysis*

---

The growth of distribution channels and the increase in customer support services created the need for customer profitability analysis. Cost information by customer is compared to the revenues generated from that customer. It is not uncommon to find that a relatively small number of customers provide most of the profit while the remaining customers provide little or no profit, although it is important not to be too quick to eliminate unprofitable customers. Customer relationships are generally long-term (Maher, 1997).

Furthermore, companies with more than one product should identify all the transactions of a customer before assessing that customer's profitability. For example, a bank may find that it loses money on the traditional banking transaction of a customer but more than compensates for it in foreign exchange and trust business of that customer. Management can use customer cost information to establish its strategic plan.

Activity-based costing (A.B.C.) and automated information systems made it possible to measure the profitability of each customer. A.B.C. provides the methods to assign marketing, distribution and support expenses to customers. Advances in information technology have reduced the costs of generating information on revenues and costs per customer. Professor Robert S. Kaplan demonstrates a good example of why customer profitability analysis is needed in a Harvard Business School case about the Swedish firm Kanthal.

Kanthal's selling and administrative expenses were 34 percent of total costs. Any improvements that can cut selling and administrative costs, say by 20 percent, would reduce total costs by almost 7 percent! Forty percent of Kanthal's Swedish customers generated 250 percent of its profits and the 10 percent least profitable customers lost 120 percent of the profits. Some of Kanthal's largest volume customers were not profitable. Identifying why certain customers were unprofitable enabled Kanthal to either make those customers profitable or get rid of them.

Cooper & Kaplan (1998) argued that the assignment of selling, marketing, distribution and administrative expenses to customers is valuable because customers do not use these resources equally. It enables a firm to measure customers' profitability, identify which customers are too expensive to serve, and to design a strategy toward each customer. The authors classified customers into four groups: high-profit and low-cost to serve, high-profit and high-costs to serve, low-profit and low-cost to serve, and low-profit and high-cost to serve.

For high-cost customers, the first step is to determine the cause of the high cost. Maybe the customer is new and most of the costs may be due to developing the relationship, costs that will be reduced in the future. If it is due to the customer ordering customized products in small quantities with unpredictable schedules, the firm may work with the customer to change his behavior. The firm may also be able to improve internally and coordinate with the customer to lower the cost of serving him.

For high-cost, low-margin customers who are not willing to work with the firm to reduce the cost of service, the firm may add a surcharge for the special services it provides. If the margin on sales to expensive customers are high enough to justify the high cost, then the firm can continue providing the same level of service.

For low-cost, high-margin customers, the firm may have to offer price discounts to keep them. Cooper & Kaplan (1998) noted that Wal-Mart used its purchasing system, which reduces the cost of service to its suppliers, to negotiate favorable terms with them.

Related to customer profitability is marketing channel profitability. The variety of channels of distribution has increased tremendously. Each type of channel has its own demands on the resources of a firm, such as price discounts, deliveries, joint promotions, return policy and credit terms. Channel profitability analysis is very useful in allocating marketing resources and focusing efforts.

# KEY 11

## *Relevant costs for managerial decisions*

---

**M**anagers have to choose between making or buying components and services, and replacing or continuing to use equipment and facilities. But before making a choice, managers must know the relevant costs for each. Relevant costs are the estimated future costs that differ among alternatives. There are several ways to identify relevant costs.

Differential cost is the difference in total costs between two alternatives. An example of differential cost is the difference between the cost of making a component and the price of buying it.

Opportunity cost is the maximum available contribution to profit that is lost by using limited resources for a specific purpose. For example, if a part is outsourced, the machine or space that would have been used for making the part internally can be used to make another product. The contribution by this other product is an opportunity cost of continuing to make the component internally.

Sunk cost is the expenditure made in the past that cannot be changed by present or future decisions. For example, the cost of a piece of equipment that can no longer be returned for a full refund is a sunk cost that is not relevant for the decision to buy a new replacement.

> **Life and money — you can't separate them. Not on this planet. Not in the kind of life you have to live.**

*Thomas H. Radal,* A Muster to Arms

### MAKE-OR-BUY DECISIONS

The make-or-buy decision is to either make a part or component in-house or source it from an outside supplier. The only costs compared to the purchase price are costs that can be eliminated if the component is bought from a supplier.

Example: Seow's company makes 50,000 valves annually that are used in several of its products. The following are the full costs of those valves:

| | |
|---|---|
| Direct materials | $200,000 |
| Direct labor | 250,000 |
| Variable overhead | 125,000 |
| Fixed overhead | 175,000 |
| Total costs | $750,000 |

An outside supplier offered to sell Seow 50,000 valves at $14 per valve (i.e., $700,000 for the 50,000 valves). The fixed overhead costs include $35,000 the salary of the supervisor of the valve operation. The supervisor will be reassigned if the valves are out-sourced. The machines used to make the valves can be used to expand the output of product X and would result in $100,000 profit.

Should Seow accept the supplier's offer or continue to make the valves internally?

Cost savings if the valves are out-sourced:

| | |
|---|---|
| Direct materials | $200,000 |
| Direct labor | 250,000 |
| Variable overhead | 125,000 |
| Supervisor's salary | 35,000 |
| Opportunity cost (profit of product X) | 100,000 |
| Total costs saved | $710,000 |
| Supplier's price | 700,000 |
| Savings if out-sourced | $10,000 |

Qualitative factors, such as the reputation of a supplier, can help influence quantitative decisions. Factors such as the supplier's ability to meet performance standards on time are critical to success. Some businesses certify suppliers. A certified supplier is a specially selected supplier who is assured a high level of business for conforming to high standards for quality and delivery schedules

### ASSETS REPLACEMENT DECISIONS
Firms are always faced with the decision of re-

placing equipment. The most difficult part in the decision is treating the book value of the existing equipment as a sunk cost that has no relevance to the decision. The issue is complicated because financial accounting requires writing off any book loss from the disposal of the asset.

For example, the Noah Company is considering replacing an old machine with a new, more efficient machine. Data on the machines follows:

| | |
|---|---|
| **New machine:** | |
| Price new | $300,000 |
| Annual variable expenses | $150,000 |
| Expected life | 4 years |
| | |
| **Old machine:** | |
| Original cost | $250,000 |
| Remaining book value | $200,000 |
| Disposal value now | $50,000 |
| Annual variable expenses | $220,000 |
| Remaining life | 4 years |

Noah Company's sales are $500,000 per year and fixed expenses (other than depreciation) are $90,000 per year. Should the new machine be purchased?

Incorrect solution: Some managers would not purchase the new machine because disposal of the old machine would apparently result in a loss:

| | |
|---|---|
| Remaining book value | $200,000 |
| Disposal value now | $50,000 |
| Loss from disposal | $150,000 |

Correct Solution: The remaining book value of the old machine is a sunk cost that cannot be avoided by the company. This can be shown by looking at comparative cost and revenue data for the next five years taken together:

|  | **5 Years Together** | | |
| | **Keep Old Machine** | **Purchase New Machine** | **Differential Costs** |
| Sales | $2,000,000 | $2,000,000 | $— |
| Variable expenses | (880,000) | (600,000) | 280,000 |
| Other fixed expenses | (360,000) | (360,000) | — |
| Cost of new machine | — | (300,000) | (300,000) |
| Disposal value of old machine | — | 50,000 | 50,000 |
| Total net income | $760,000 | $790,000 | $30,000 |

Using only relevant costs, the solution would be:

| | |
|---|---|
| Savings in variable expenses provided by the new machine ($220,000 − $150,000) × 4 yrs. | $280,000 |
| Cost of the new machine | ($300,000) |
| Disposal value of the old machine | $50,000 |
| Net advantage of the new machine | $30,000 |

**SUMMARY**

A manager should follow the steps below in identifying the costs (and revenues) that are relevant in a decision:

◆ Assemble all of the costs and revenues associated with each alternative.
◆ Eliminate those costs that are sunk.
◆ Eliminate those costs and revenues that do not differ between alternatives.
◆ Make a decision based on the remaining costs and revenues. These are the costs and revenues that are different, or avoidable, and hence relevant to making the decision.

# KEY 12

## Pricing and product mix analysis

Setting prices of products and services is complex and is influenced by many factors. A firm can be a price-taker or a price-setter. A price-taker has little or no influence on the industry supply and demand, and, consequently, on the prices of its products. A price-taker must simply sell as many of its products as possible as long as its costs are less than its prices. A price-setter can set the prices of its products because it has a significant market share in its industry.

Another factor influencing prices is the increasingly short product life cycle. Firms develop prices based on forecasted product life cycle revenues and costs.

### SHORT AND LONG-RUN PRICING DECISIONS
Short-term pricing decisions are different from long-term decisions. In the short-term, a firm with excess capacity may be willing to accept prices below full cost. In the long run, managers have more flexibility in adjusting the capacities of

resources to match demand for resources. Furthermore, in the long-term, prices must exceed full cost if the firm is to survive.

### SHORT-RUN PRICING DECISIONS
In the short-term, a firm is faced with two types of pricing decisions. The first is the product mix when it faces a capacity constraint and the second is special-order pricing when it has excess capacity.

Most companies are capable of producing a large variety of goods and services, but may be limited in the short run by available capacity. Firms often face the problem of deciding how scarce resources are going to be used. For example, a particular machine may not have enough capacity to satisfy the demand for all of the company's products. In such cases, the important measure of profitability is the contribution margin per unit of the scarce resource, not contribution margin per unit of product. However, the final decision may be affected by policy considerations, such as maintaining a full product line.

Example: Mona Company manufactures two products, P and Q:

|  | P | Q |
|---|---|---|
| Selling price per unit | $12 | $10 |
| Less variable expenses per unit | 08 | 07 |
| Contribution margin | $04 | $03 |
|  |  |  |
| Contribution margin ratio | 33% | 30% |
| Current demand per week (units) | 1,800 | 2,400 |
| Processing time required per unit | .5 min. | .6 min. |
| Total minutes required | 900 min. | 1,440 min. |

The process has 2,100 minutes capacity per week, which is not enough capacity to satisfy demand for both product P and product Q. Should the company focus its efforts on product P or product Q?

The contribution margin per unit of the scarce resource:

| | P | Q |
|---|---|---|
| Contribution margin per unit (a) | $04 | $03 |
| Time required to produce one unit (b) | .5 min. | .6 min. |
| Contribution margin per minute (a)/(b) | $8/min. | $5/min. |

All units of product P should be produced because it has a higher contribution per minute than product Q:

| | | |
|---|---|---|
| Total capacity in minutes | | 2,100 min. |
| Product P | 1,800 units × .5 min | 900 min |
| Available capacity | | 1,200 min |
| Minutes per unit of Q | | ÷ .6 min. |
| Total units of Q | | 2,000 units |

## DIFFERENTIAL PRICING

If a firm has excess capacity, it may consider accepting orders at prices below its current prices. In such cases, incremental revenues have to be greater than incremental costs. Incremental costs (or revenues) are the amount by which costs (or revenues) change as a result of the special order. Such price differential may also be used if the firm's products have peak periods. To rationalize the demand for its products, a firm may offer lower prices for off-peak demand.

There are two caveats for differential pricing. First, the firm's current customers may find out about the lower prices and demand to pay the same. The second is that competitors may claim that different prices are predatory and intended to drive them out of the market. Predatory prices are against Federal laws that promote fair competition.

## PRICING STRATEGIES

The strength of demand for the product determines the pricing strategy a firm will use. If demand is high, a firm can have a higher markup. If demand is elastic, a small increase in price results in a large decrease in demand. Hence, markups are lower when demand is elastic.

The level of competition also affects pricing strategy. When competition is intense, markups decrease and firms find it is hard to sustain prices much higher than their incremental costs.

Firms also may follow skimming or penetrating pricing strategies. Skimming pricing strategy charges a higher price initially from customers willing to pay more for the privilege of possessing a new product. Penetration pricing strategy is where a lower price is charged initially to win over market share from an established product of a competitor.

## LONG-RUN MIX DECISIONS

Decisions to add new, or drop, products often have long-term implications for the cost structure of the firm. Committed costs cannot be easily changed in the short-run, so changing the product mix cannot be done quickly. Furthermore, there can only be cost savings if the resources required to support the dropped product could be eliminated or redeployed. Another consideration is that some customers may want a firm to maintain a full product line so that they do not have to go elsewhere. Thus, some unprofitable products may be kept to maintain the entire product line.

# KEY 13

## Budgeting and control

A budget is a plan describing the use and source of financial and operating resources over a given time period. It includes financial plans of revenues and expenditures needed to carry out the organization's tasks and meet its financial goals. Budgets help managers decide if their goals can be achieved and, if not, what modifications are needed. By comparing actual results with the budget, managers can take corrective action. Finally, a budget assists in planning, motivation, evaluation and control, communication, coordination and education.

### THE BUDGETARY CYCLE

- ◆ Provides a frame of reference with specific expectations.
- ◆ Plans the performance for the firm and its subunits.
- ◆ Investigates variations from plans and take corrective actions.
- ◆ Plans again, using feedback and new constraints.

## BENEFITS OF BUDGETS

◆ Forces managers to plan ahead and think about long-term strategies.
◆ Provides performance criteria.
◆ Promotes communication and coordination.
◆ A control tool.

## MASTER BUDGET

The master budget summarizes goals of all sub-units: sales, production, marketing, customer service, and finance. A master budget consists of:

| Operating budget | Financial budget |
|---|---|
| Sales budget | Capital budget |
| Production budget | Cash budget |
| Factory overhead budget | Budgeted balance sheet |
| Marketing expense budget | Budgeted income statement |
| Administrative expense budget | |

## PREPARING AN OPERATING BUDGET

Forecast sales for the sales budget. Forecasting methods include polling sales staff, statistical approaches and executives group judgment. Several factors affecting future sales include: state of the economy and industry; stage of product life cycle; pricing and competition; advertising and promotions; sales force quality; and production capacity.

Prepare a production budget based on the sales budget and the firm's inventory policy. From the production budget, prepare the following:

| | |
|---|---|
| direct materials usage budget | marketing and administrative |
| expense budget | direct labor budget |
| factory overhead budget | ending inventory budget |
| cost-of-goods-sold budget | budgeted income statement |
| budgeted balance sheet | cash budget |

## FLEXIBLE BUDGET

Master budgets are prepared for a single activity level. It is difficult to evaluate actual operating results when actual activity differs from the planned level of activity. Comparing the master budgets with actual results is like comparing apples and oranges. An *ex post* budget is prepared to show revenues and expenses that should have occurred at the actual activity. The budget for the actual volume is called a flexible budget because it is based on costs behavior, (i.e., variable and fixed costs. Total variable costs change in direct proportion to changes in activity.) Total fixed costs remain unchanged within the relevant range.

Flexible budget = (Budgeted variable cost/unit × actual units) + Budgeted fixed costs

The benefits of the flexible budget are that it reveals variances due to good cost control or lack of cost control and is useful in performance evaluation.

Here's an illustration:

The Hala Company makes and sells a product at $20 per unit. Forecasted sales for the period are 10,000 units. Budgeted costs are: variable manufacturing cost per unit, $6; budgeted manufacturing fixed cost, $20,000; variable selling expenses (commission), 1 percent of sales revenue, and budgeted fixed selling and administrative costs, $15,000. Actual results: 9,000 units sold; revenue, $198,000; variable manufacturing costs, $58,500; fixed manufacturing costs, $18,200; variable marketing expenses, $19,800, and fixed selling and administrative costs, $17,000.

Solution:

| | Actual | Flexible Budget Variance | Flexible Budget | Master Budget Variance | Master Budget |
|---|---|---|---|---|---|
| Units | 9,000 | | 9,000 | 1,000 | 10,000 |
| Revenue | $198,000 | $18,000 | $180,000 | ($20,000) | $200,000 |
| Variable costs: | | | | | |
| Manufacturing | 58,000 | (4,000) | 54,000 | 6,000 | 60,000 |
| Marketing | 19,800 | (1,800) | 18,000 | 2,000 | 20,000 |
| Total | 77,800 | (5,800) | 72,000 | 8,000 | 80,000 |
| Contribution margin | 120,200 | 12,200 | 108,000 | 12,000 | 120,000 |
| Fixed costs: | | | | | |
| Manufacturing | 18,200 | 1,800 | 20,000 | 0 | 20,000 |
| S & A | 17,000 | (2,000) | 15,000 | 0 | 15,000 |
| Total | 35,200 | (200) | 35,000 | 0 | 35,000 |
| Operating profit | $85,000 | $12,000 | $73,000 | ($12,000) | $85,000 |

Although the master budgeted profit and actual profit are equal, $85,000, the actual activities are different from the budgeted activities. A flexible budget would reveal where there are differences between the master budget activities and the actual activities.

The comparison of the flexible budget with the master budget shows that the decrease in volume by 1,000 units should have reduced the operating profit by $12,000. However, the comparison of the flexible budget with the actual results shows that the increase in selling price resulted in $18,000 in revenue, but that there are increases in costs. This gives management more useful information.

# KEY 14

## Cash management

C ash management is critical to the survival of organizations. Many small firms go out of business when their sales grow because of poor cash management. As a firm's sales start to grow, it has more bills to collect from its customers and more payments to make to its suppliers. If the firm is poorly managed and does not timely process and collect revenues from its customers, it may run out of cash to pay its suppliers and be forced to go out of business.

Billing customers and collecting receivables in a timely manner may reduce a firm's capital requirement. Processing and paying suppliers' bills on time can reduce a firm's costs. A cash budget based on sound cash flow analysis is a useful managerial tool. The cash budget will identify when extra cash will be needed (borrowing needs) and when there will be sufficient cash to repay a loan. A cash break-even analysis helps a manager estimate the sales level at which enough cash inflow is generated to meet cash outflow commitments.

$$\text{Cash break-even} = \frac{\text{Fixed cash costs}}{\text{Cash contribution per unit}}$$

## CASH PLANNING AND CONTROL

The objectives of a cash policy are to maximize liquidity by making the best use of liquid assets while minimizing risks. Since idle cash does not contribute to the profits and growth of the business, a firm should strive to reduce the cash balance as much as possible. On the other hand, a firm should keep enough cash to:

◆ Take advantage of trade discounts
◆ Maintain a good credit rating in trade
◆ Retain sufficient funds for business opportunities
◆ Be prepared for emergencies
◆ Meet anticipated seasonal needs

To achieve the apparently opposing objectives of maintaining enough cash while minimizing idle cash, a firm can strive to accelerate its flow of cash. It can do this by:

◆ Eliminating delays from the time a product is shipped until the payment is received. Most delays are caused by paperwork bottlenecks.
◆ Processing high-dollar invoices first.
◆ Billing a customer for each shipment separately and not waiting until all orders of that customer are shipped before billing him.
◆ Analyzing the delivery system for invoices. If the regular mail takes too long it may be necessary to use a faster delivery system for high-dollar invoices.
◆ Reviewing the internal credit policies to determine whether the business is losing money because the credit policies are either too stringent or too loose. A business

may consider using credit cards as an alternative, or selling (factoring) its accounts receivable.

◆ Offering prompt payment discounts.

◆ Timing the deposits to reach the bank before the cut-off period for the current day so they will be entered in that day's receipts.

◆ Speeding up action on delinquent accounts.

◆ Using bank services such as a lock box that permits cash to be deposited before the bookkeeping has been completed and wire transfers that provide instant point-to-point credit. It is necessary, though, to watch out for the cost of the bank services.

◆ Taking advantage of vendors' terms either by taking the cash discount or waiting for the maximum allowed period to pay the bill.

◆ Managing the net float efficiently. The net float is the difference between a firm's disbursement and its deposits float. The disbursement float is caused by the time lag between the time a check is written and subtracted from the cash balance in the firm's books and the time it is subtracted from the firm's account at the bank. Deposit float is the time lag between the time of entering a deposit in the firm's books until the deposit is credited to its bank account.

◆ Optimizing cash utilization. Firms can do this by efficient management of working capital (e.g., no excessive inventories).

They can also do it by investing excess cash, even temporary excess cash using sources of short-term money, and maintain good relations with these sources; performing cash forecasting; forecasting cash receipts and disbursements, and forecasting revenues in terms of cash collections and not sales.

If business is cyclical, recognize the peaks and valleys by making monthly projections; projecting your expenditures in terms of payments, for a corresponding period, and planning what investments will be made for capital assets and the probable timing of the payment for such investments. Based on the projections of receipts and disbursements, determine the availability of excess cash or the anticipated cash deficit on a monthly basis.

Traditional methods of cash forecasting usually assume values with certainty, when in reality the expected results are subject to a margin of error. Financial simulation, on the other hand, allows one to incorporate both future uncertainty and the many variable interrelationships in the study. Simulation can be used to study how a cash budget is affected if some of the input variables in the model are modified or subjected to random variation. For example, one can treat the collection rate as a random variable with a certain mean and a standard deviation. The same can be assumed for sales or any other variable.

### RELATING OPERATING BUDGETS TO CASH
Traditionally, budget preparation starts with sales, then other operating budgets and finally the cash budget is prepared based on the flows expected from the operating budgets. This approach assumes that the firm will be able to finance any cash needs form external sources. In reality, many cash-strapped small businesses have no external sources of funds and may have to finance all their cash needs from internal sources. In such businesses, availability of cash has a significant influence on operating plans. The separation of the two activities, especially in expanding a small business, has caused many to fold.

Spradlin, et al. (1976), developed some decision

rules that help the person preparing the budget focus on the interrelation between cash and the key operating budgets. According to the decision rules, each dollar of cash received during a period and each dollar of expected sales in the next period represent a potential constraint on current cash disbursements. For example: cash disbursements for merchandise should be the lesser of cost of merchandise sold as a percentage of sales times next period's expected sales.

Illustration 1:

| | |
|---|---|
| Current year receipts | $150,000 |
| Expected sales next year | 200,000 |
| Cost of merchandise sold as percentage of sales | 65% |

1. Merchandise sold as percentage of sales receipts of current period
   $150,000 × .65 = $97,500
2. Merchandise sold as percentage of sales times expected next year's sales
   $200,000 × .65 = $130,000

Decision: disbursements for merchandise should not exceed $97,500

Illustration 2:

| | |
|---|---|
| Current year's receipts | $150,000 |
| Expected sales next year | 100,000 |
| Merchandise sold as percentage of sales | 65% |

1. Merchandise sold as a percentage of sales times current year receipts
   $150,000 × .65 = $97,500
2. Merchandise sold as percentage of sales times expected next year's sales
   $100,000 × .65 = $65,000

Decision: disbursements for merchandise should not exceed $65,000.

With this decision rule, merchandise inventory next year will not increase simply because next year's sales are expected to increase. Any increase has to be decided by management based on the availability of external sources of cash. On the other hand, if next year's sales are expected to be less than the current year's receipts, then inventory is automatically decreased. Similar decision rules can be used for labor and all other items that require disbursements.

| Cash Flow Schedule | | | | | |
|---|---|---|---|---|---|
| | Jul | Aug | Sep | Oct | Nov |
| **Estimated Receipts** | | | | | |
| Cash sales | $800 | $600 | $700 | $1,200 | $2,800 |
| Accounts receivable | 10,000 | 10,000 | 15,800 | 20,000 | 31,600 |
| Other income | 200 | 400 | 200 | 480 | 250 |
| Total receipts | $11,000 | $11,200 | $16,700 | $21,680 | $34,650 |
| | | | | | |
| **Estimated Disbursements** | | | | | |
| Accounts payable | 17,000 | 11,000 | 8,200 | 2,700 | 2,200 |
| Payroll & drawing | 2,600 | 4,200 | 4,200 | 7,900 | 5,800 |
| Expense | 1,200 | 1,800 | 2,000 | 2,700 | 600 |
| Interest expense | 130 | 130 | 130 | 130 | 130 |
| Plant & equipment | 2,500 | 460 | 600 | 800 | 100 |
| Reserve for taxes | | | | *3,800 | *3,800 |
| Total disbursements | $23,430 | $17,590 | $15,130 | $18,030 | $12,630 |
| Estimated excess | | | | | |
| receipts over | | | | | |
| disbursements | ($12,430) | ($6,390) | $1,570 | $3,650 | $22,020 |
| Estimated cash balance | | | | | |
| at start of month | $4,200 | $7,770 | $1,380 | $2,950 | $6,600 |
| Borrowings | $16000 | | | | |
| Loan repayment | | | | | $16,000 |
| Estimated cash balance | | | | | |
| at end of month | $7,770 | $1,380 | $2,950 | $6,600 | $12,620 |

\* To be allotted October and November so that available cash can be kept at the maximum during the months of heavy cash outflows.

# KEY 15

## *Capital budgeting*

A capital budget is a large outlay of resources to acquire long-term assets such as plant and equipment. Usually, capital investment resources are scarce, so there must be a way to select from among competing requests for limited funds. Traditional investment analysis tools may not be adequate to make these types of decisions. The day-to-day operating impact may not be the key factor in making a decision. Less tangible benefits may be the deciding factor in whether to invest in new technology. Hence, capital budgeting should be linked to the strategic objectives of the organization. Discounted methods, such as net present value and internal rate of return, explicitly consider the time value of money. Non-discounted methods, such as payback and accounting rate of return, ignore time value of money.

### SIX STAGES IN CAPITAL BUDGETING
- ◆ Identify projects that satisfy organizational objectives

- Search among projects, exploring specific investments
- Collect information on alternative investments
- Select projects using various methods
- Secure financing for selected projects
- Implement and control

### METHODS FOR PROJECT EVALUATION

There are two types of project evaluation methods. The discounted cash flow methods of the net present value and the internal rate of return, which incorporate the time value of money. The other methods ignore the time value of money. These are the payback and the accrual accounting rate of return methods. Before evaluating the projects, you should consider the following items:

- Initial investment
- Disposal value of old plant/equipment
- Recurring operating cash flows
- Terminal value of investment
- Effect of income taxes
- Inflation effects
- Risk

### DISCOUNTED CASH FLOW METHODS

Net Present Value (N.P.V.): the difference between the present values of expected cash receipts and cash outlays for the project. The cash flows are discounted using the firm's cost of capital rate.

Accept project if its N.P.V. > 0

Internal Rate of Return (I.R.R.): the rate that equates expected cash receipts and cash outlays for the project.

Accept project if its I.R.R. > R.R.R. (Required rate of return)

Payback method: the payback period is the time it takes to recover invested funds. The payback period ignores time value of money and profitability.

Accrual Accounting Rate-of-Return method: measures the increase in expected average annual operating income divided by net initial investment, and considers profitability, but ignores the time value of money.

## COMPLEXITIES IN CAPITAL BUDGETING

There are risks and uncertainty in forecasting the details of a capital project over its life of several years. Unforeseen changes in the environment may result in the project taking longer or costing more than what is forecasted. Its actual cash flows may differ from the projections. One way to recognize the risks and uncertainty is to perform sensitivity analysis. At least three alternatives can be considered: An optimistic alternative that assumes the best possible results for the project; a pessimistic alternative that assumes all that can go wrong with the project will go wrong, and a realistic alternative that represents the consensus of the people preparing the capital budget. The realistic alternative is what will be used in approving and implementing the project, but the other two alternatives help management see the risks and potentials of each project and may help in choosing between two competing projects.

There are qualitative factors that may have a significant impact on the success of a capital project. For example, the flexibility to make changes in the project during the implementation stage. Another important factor is the response of the employees to the project. Are they embracing or resisting the project?

Here's an illustration of the different methods of analyzing capital projects: A consulting firm is considering three microcomputer networking proposals for its Boston and Hartford offices. All three proposals have an estimated useful life of three years and estimated salvage value of zero.

| | Proposal X | Proposal Y | Proposal Z |
|---|---|---|---|
| Initial investment in equipment | $45,000 | $45,000 | $45,000 |
| Annual cash increase in operations: | | | |
| Year 1 | $40,000 | $22,500 | $15,000 |
| Year 2 | $5,000 | $22,500 | $20,000 |
| Year 3 | $22,500 | $22,500 | $30,000 |

The table below lists the results and ranking of each of the three proposals using each of the four different methods of analysis:

| Methods of analysis | Proposal X | Proposal Y | Proposal Z |
|---|---|---|---|
| Net present value (N.P.V.) | $10,715 | $9,041 | $5,690 |
| Proposal ranking | 1 | 2 | 3 |
| | | | |
| Internal rate of return (I.R.R.) | 28% | 23% | 18% |
| Proposal ranking | 1 | 2 | 3 |
| | | | |
| Payback period | 2 years | 2 years | 2.33 years |
| Proposal ranking | 1 | 1 | 3 |
| | | | |
| Accrual accounting rate of return | 16.7% | 16.7% | 14.8% |
| Proposal ranking | 1 | 1 | 3 |

Proposals X and Z are ranked 1 and 3, respectively, by all four methods. However, the payback method and the accrual accounting rate of return failed to distinguish between proposals X and Y, even though the two proposals have different streams of cash flows. This can be attributed to both methods ignoring the time value of money. Hence, N.P.V. and I.R.R. are preferred because they take into consideration the time value of money.

# KEY 16

## Control in an age of empowerment

It has been argued that employee empowerment is critical to an organization's success. Employee empowerment is defined as giving workers the power to make decisions without waiting for approval from superiors. Employee empowerment creates risks that require different systems of control. The traditional hierarchical command and control system is no longer adequate. It has to be augmented by other systems.

Robert Simon of Harvard University (1995) proposed adding three more control systems: a belief system that is value-laden and inspirational, which should be advocated and followed by senior management; a boundary control system that clearly identifies areas and actions that are off-limit. For example, bribing government officials. A code of conduct is an example of a boundary control system, and finally, an interactive system that keeps employees alert to changes in the environment that may present potential opportunities or problems to the organization. For example, PepsiCo follows closely demographic trends because they affect demand for its products.

### DIAGNOSTIC CONTROL SYSTEMS

Diagnostic control systems include budgeting, standards and quotas. One of the objectives of these systems is to reduce constant monitoring by managers and allow the practice of management by exception, where managers attend only to out-of-control processes. However, the pressures to meet budgets, standards or quotas increases the potential for control failures. The literature is replete with cases of employees manipulating results or engaging in dysfunctional behavior. A recent example is Sears' repair centers case, which cost Sears $60 million.

Diagnostic control systems need to be supplemented with other control systems.

### BELIEFS SYSTEMS

Simon describes belief systems as value-laden and inspirational. They include firms' mottoes and credos. They tend to be broad and lack substance. For belief systems to be effective control systems, senior managers' actions should match them. An example of an effective belief system is the Johnson & Johnson Credo, which served the firm admirably well during the Tylenol case.

### BOUNDARY SYSTEMS

These systems explicitly set the boundaries between acceptable and unacceptable behavior. They usually include written policies and procedures such as codes of conduct. They may include both ethical and strategic boundaries. An example of an ethical boundary is where consulting firms prohibit employees from revealing any information about clients, not even names of clients to spouses. An example of strategic boundaries is where a firm prohibits employees from accepting certain types of business. For example, some firms will not pursue projects that may have potential environmental or ethical problems.

### INTERACTIVE CONTROL SYSTEMS

These are sensing systems that help a firm detect changes in the environment that may affect its operations. Firms track strategic uncertainties related to their markets, including technologies, regulations and political developments. PepsiCo tracks demographic trends because they affect the demand for its products.

**For which of you, intending to build a tower, sitteth not down first and counteth the cost, whether he have sufficient to finish it?**

*New Testament: Luke*

# KEY 17

## Target costing and value engineering

The Japanese have developed several management tools that helped them achieve global success. Three of them are target costing, value engineering and the survival triplet.

Target costing is a management tool for reducing the overall cost of a product over its entire life cycle with the help of the production, engineering, R&D, marketing, and accounting departments as well as suppliers. The first step in target costing is determining the target price. Target price is what customers are willing to pay. The target cost is calculated as the difference between the target price and the desired profit. The organization uses value engineering and the survival triplet to achieve the target cost.

Target costing is the discipline that insures that new products are profitable when they are launched. That is:

Target Cost = Target Price − Target Margin

#### Characteristics of target costing

- Used at planning and design stages.
- Cost planning and not cost control tool.
- More useful in manufacturing.
- Helps in control of design specification and production techniques.

#### Tools used in target costing

- Value engineering (V.E.) is a systematic, cross-functional examination of factors that affect the cost of a product to find ways to achieve the specified purpose, at the required standards of quality and reliability, at the target cost.
- Just-In-Time.
- Total quality management.

#### Setting target costing

- The target price of a new product is determined primarily from market analysis.
- The target margin is determined from corporate profit expectations, historical results, competitive analysis, and, sometimes, computer simulations.
- The new product's target price is used as the basis for determining the purchase price of components and raw materials acquired externally.
- Target costing is characterized by the intensity with which the rule "the target cost can never be exceeded" is applied. In practice, of course, the "never exceeded" rule is broken at times, but the conditions must justify it and specified procedures must be followed to authorize it.

#### Steps in cost reduction

- Breakdown the product into its components and assign the target cost of each.
- Estimate the cost of each component.

- Identify where estimated costs exceed target cost.
- Assemble teams from marketing, finance, design, manufacturing and suppliers to review costs and work toward achieving target cost.
- Use V.E. and survival triplet to achieve target cost.
- If target cost cannot be achieved, renegotiate price or drop product.

Watch out, target costing can have several unintended consequences:

- Conflict between different departments in the allocation of total costs between different functions and components.
- Employee burnout from the constant pressure to meet the target cost.
- Supplier fatigue.

### VALUE ENGINEERING

The objective of value engineering is to eliminate waste and make products that best suit customers' needs. It's an approach in which the members of a multidisciplinary team work together during the design phase to find ways to trim costs before the manufacturing stage.

- V.E. is applied during the design phase of product development.
- V.E. is a team-based approach. Teams sometimes include suppliers and subcontractors.
- V.E. helps a firm manage the tradeoff between functionality, quality, and cost.
- V.E. requires that each product's basic and secondary functions be identified and their values analyzed.
- The primary objective of value engineering

programs is not to minimize the cost of products, but to achieve a specified level of cost reduction (the product's target cost).

## THE SURVIVAL TRIPLET

The survival triplet is composed of three critical success factors. Cost-Price represents the cost of production or price, charged. There is a minimum the company can charge and still make a profit, but there is also a maximum amount the customer will be willing to pay. Functionality represents the product's characteristics measured on a number of dimensions. A company can add as much functionality as it wants, but there is a minimum level of functionality a customer will accept. Quality represents conformance to specifications of the product defined along the functionality axis. Identifying the maximum and minimum levels for each of the three factors helps a firm make trade-offs between them.

A firm may decide to reduce functionality to meet its target cost or make two versions of the product: one with maximum functionality and the other with the minimum. For example, a firm can make a television with the picture-in-picture feature or without it.

**The Survival Zone**
*Source: Cooper, 1994*

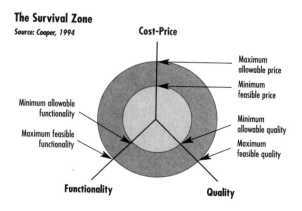

# KEY 18

## Benchmarking and kaizen

enchmarking and kaizen are two Japanese practices that are being adopted by many U.S. companies. Benchmarking identifies an activity that needs to be improved and finds an organization that is the most efficient at this activity. Firms will study the organization, and then use its process. Firms do not always benchmark the best in a business. They benchmark processes and activities that are strategically important.

Kaizen is continuous improvement resulting in greater levels of quality and lower costs. It projects costs based on future improvements rather than current practices and methods. Rather than standards or targets, the goal is current costs that are less than previous costs.

### BENCHMARKING GUIDELINES
- ◆ Do not benchmark everything that is the best. No firm can be the best at everything.
- ◆ Only benchmark the best in activities that are strategically important.

- Look for internal, regional, or industry benchmarks for less important activities.

- Product Performance—How well do our products perform compared to our competitors?
- Employee Performance—How well do our employees perform compared to our competitors?
- New Product/Service Development—Are we as innovative as our competitors?
- Cost Performance—Are our costs as low as our competitors?

## METHODS OF INFORMATION GATHERING
- Through trade associations and other publicly available sources.
- Cooperative sharing of information with other firms. This has increased as firms determined that the benefits of sharing exceed the risk of revealing proprietary information.
- Third party such as consultants who can provide information without revealing the identity of the firms.

## KAIZEN

The aim of a kaizen program is to remove inefficiencies from a firm's production process. A kaizen program typically does not focus on individual products, because it is expensive to try to reduce inefficiencies for just one product. As a kaizen program achieves its objectives, the overall cost of production and product costs fall. Thus, kaizen focuses on the production process, not on individual products.

- Cost reductions during the manufacturing cycle usually are modest because of the use of target costing in the product development stage.

- ◆ Different from standard costing because the goal is not to meet a standard but to achieve cost reductions from last period's costs. Workers are given the responsibility to reduce costs.
- ◆ Kaizen should not be used if the costs of disruptions to the process are high.

Cooper (1994) reported the following on the kaizen program of the Citizen Watch Company:

The focus of Citizen's kaizen program was the reduction of labor. The small size of Citizen's product caused the labor content of the product to be high (because material content was so low). This high labor content guided the focus of the kaizen program. The major way to reduce labor was by altering the time required to operate or support the production machines. There were two major approaches to reduction of machine time. First was to increase the running speed of the machines; increasing the running speed allowed more parts per hour to be produced. Second, find ways to increase the number of machines a single employee could operate.

The primary outcome of Citizen's kaizen program was a highly automated plant. The labor content of the product and hence its cost had fallen continuously over an extended period of time. The result of the program was to considerably reduce the number of people involved in production. In 1972, 2,952 people were required; by 1980 it was down to 2,520, and by 1990 it had fallen to 1,542, which was an overall reduction of almost 50 percent, though the number of units produced and subcontracting to subsidiaries must be taken into consideration.

# KEY 19

## Managing costs across the entire supply chain

To compete successfully, a firm must become an expert at developing low-cost and high-quality products or services that customers demand. To achieve high quality at low cost, all firms in the supply chain must have high quality and low cost. Hence, a company can not be isolated from its suppliers and customers during the design process. Barriers to communication must be overcome to promote cooperation. Inter-organizational cost management systems enable the entire supply chain to be efficient. Alliances are formed across organizational boundaries for sharing cost information to develop an efficient supply chain.

### OBJECTIVES

The goal of managing throughout the supply chain is more innovative products, faster product development, and lower costs by achieving the following objectives:

◆ Reduce time, increase functionality, improve quality, and reduce costs.

- Create relationships that lead to sharing of organizational resources, including information that helps improve inter-firm activities.
- Mechanisms for information sharing include joint R&D projects, placing of employees of one firm in others, and establishing inter-organizational cost management systems.

## A man without money is

## a bow without arrows.

***Thomas Fuller*, Gnomologia**

Shank and Govindarajan (1993) gave the following examples of the benefits of managing the supply chain:

Suppliers linkages: "When bulk chocolate began to be delivered in liquid form in tank cars instead of 10-pound molded bars, the supplier eliminated the cost of molding bars and packing them, and the confectionery producer saved the costs of unpacking and melting."

Linkages with customers: "Some container producers have constructed manufacturing facilities next to breweries and deliver containers directly onto a customer's line."

Linkages within business units: For example, product design has a great impact on production. Kamakura'a forging process helped the finishing process by redesigning molds so that less metal had to be removed to finish the part (Cooper, 1994).

Linkages across business units: For example, Proctor & Gamble's business units (disposable diapers, soap, etc.) whose products go through supermarkets share distribution with each other.

### SUPPLIERS MANAGEMENT

The benefits of long-term supplier relations include technological innovation, shared risk of high development costs, and avoiding vertical integration in a rapidly changing environment.

Outsourcing may have some added costs and risks:

◆ Additional costs will include coordination costs and transaction costs (e.g., costs of identifying suppliers and of entering and enforcing contracts).
◆ Long-term outsourcing contracts may ignore declining future marginal costs.
◆ Additional risks will include financial stability of the supplier and the potential for the breach of proprietary information.
◆ There is also a risk of being cut off from information on market, costs, and new technologies.

Before outsourcing, a firm should:

◆ Understand all aspects of production, transaction and coordination costs.
◆ Avoid outsourcing decisions based on short-term cost and cash-flow consideration.
◆ Assess impact on core competencies, technological and human.

◆ Assess the potential of suppliers ending up competing with it.

## THE SUCCESS OF CHRYSLER SUPPLY-CHAIN STRATEGY

A *Harvard Business Review* article (Dyer, 1996) describes the success of Chrysler's supply-chain strategy, calling it an American kieretsu, which is a Japanese term for a closely associated group of companies. Chrysler's strategy included the following steps:

---

### Chrysler's Supply Chain Strategy

Cross-functional vehicle development teams:
* Help end conflicting demands and shifting priorities.
* Improve coordination and trust within Chrysler and with its suppliers.

Pre-sourcing and target costing:
* Choosing suppliers at the concept stage and giving them responsibility for designing a given component.
* Making suppliers responsible for cost, quality and on-time delivery.
* Target costing is used to work with suppliers to meet cost and functionality objectives.
* Motivate suppliers to participate in continuous improvement for the whole value-chain.

Suggestions by the suppliers that can reduce Chrysler's and the suppliers' costs:
* Number of suggestions and amounts saved were incorporated in the supplier rating system.
* Savings are shared with the supplier.

Enhance communication and coordination with suppliers:
* Resident suppliers' engineers working with Chrysler's engineers in Chrysler's facilities.
* Common E-mail.
* Advisory board of executives from the 14 top suppliers.
* Annual meeting with the top 150 strategic suppliers.

Results:
* Time to develop a vehicle reduced from 234 weeks to 160 weeks.
* Costs to develop a vehicle reduced by 20–40 percent.
* Average profits per vehicle increased from $250 to $2,110.
* Reduced the number of buyers by 30 percent.
* The assets or facilities of suppliers were dedicated to Chrysler.

---

# KEY 20

## *Performance measurement and reward systems*

Compensation is an important factor in motivation and performance. The relationship between performance measures and the reward system is very important, especially at the senior management level. The goals of such systems are:

- Incentives for better current and future performance.
- Reward past performance.
- Attract new managers.
- Retain superior managers.
- Risk sharing between managers and shareholders.
- Reduce taxes for managers and the corporation.
- Promote entrepreneurial spirit.

### ATTRIBUTES OF PERFORMANCE AND REWARD SYSTEMS
- Employees must have confidence that the performance measurement rewards performance controlled by them.
- Ideally, the performance measurement

system should measure the output of employees. However, there are situations where the output of employees is determined by factors not under their control. Where that happens, the input of employees is measured and rewarded.

◆ The system should measure and reward actions that contribute to the firm's success.
◆ The system should balance between the short-term and the long-term.
◆ There should be clear and measurable standards.
◆ Measurements should be accurate and timely.
◆ Where coordination and teamwork is necessary, the system should reflect that.

### EXAMPLES OF PERFORMANCE MEASUREMENT AND REWARD SYSTEMS

Kaplan and Atkins (1998) reported the following characteristics of a components manufacturer's system:

◆ Executive performance is measured on six attributes: quality, timeliness, cost control, sales growth, profitability and employee morale.
◆ Rewards are based on ability to meet annual targets, and relative improvement of performance over a three-year period, but the rewards are made annually.

Targets are set based on discussions between subordinates and their superiors. The discussions address the choice of standards as well as the appropriateness and controllability of the attributes being measured.

# KEY 21

## Time as a competitive factor

Success in a competitive environment depends on a shorter product-development cycle and rapid response to customers. Companies that bring new products to market faster than competitors tend to earn a premium. The Big Three U.S. auto companies worked hard to reduce their product-development cycles to compete with the Japanese.

There are four measures of time that are important: product-development cycle; customer response time, break-even time (i.e., the time it takes to recoup investment), and manufacturing cycle time (i.e., the time necessary to manufacturing a product).

### NEW PRODUCT DEVELOPMENT TIME
New product development time is the amount of time from the initial approval of the concept by management to its market introduction. Increased emphasis due to shorter product life cycles (time from the initial R&D to the withdrawal of customer support). For example:

Toyota/Honda cars = 3 years
GM/Ford/Chrysler cars = 4 years

Because Toyota/Honda cars have shorter life cycles than GM/Ford/Chrysler cars, Toyota/Honda can respond faster to changes in customers' tastes than GM/Ford/Chrysler.

Factors affecting new product development time:

◆ Project scope; complexity and number of changes.
◆ Project planning and management; concurrent design and development can reduce development time.
◆ Organizational capabilities; computer-based design and development can reduce development time.
◆ Management controls for new product development time; the management accountant's role is to develop consistent measures for the development time for new products.

### BREAK-EVEN TIME FOR NEW PRODUCTS

Break-even time (B.E.T.) is the time from when the initial concept for a new product is approved by management until the cumulative present value of net cash inflows from the project equals the cumulative present value of net investment outflows.

B.E.T. promotes aggressive efforts by personnel to speed up the time taken to get a new product to market. It is superior to the payback method because the B.E.T. incorporates the time value of money and starts counting time at the beginning of the project, irrespective of when the cash outflows occur.

The limitations of B.E.T. are that it: ignores profitability, de-emphasizes long-range thinking,  has strictly financial focus, and is not comparable across businesses.

## OPERATIONAL MEASURES OF TIME

Customer-response time is the amount of time from when a customer places an order to when the product or service is delivered. Customer-response time includes the time spent on the following steps: order processing, order manufacturing, and order delivery. The time taken for each affects competitiveness, quality and costs. Hence, managing the time of these steps is critical. This is accomplished by identifying value-adding and non-value-adding activities in each step. Try to eliminate non-value-adding activities and improve the efficiency of value-adding activities and non-value adding activities that cannot be eliminated.

**Money, the life-blood of the nations, corrupts and stagnates in the veins, unless a proper circulation its motion and heat maintains.**

*Swift*

# KEY 22

## *Total quality management*

Total quality management is a management method by which an organization seeks to excel on all dimensions, with the customer ultimately defining quality. Direct measures of quality are the number of customer complaints, percentage of on time delivery, and proportion of first-time, first-quality product. Direct measures of quality are analyzed using cause and effect analysis, control charts and Pareto Charts.

Historically, quality was considered expensive. It was believed that there is a minimum (normal) level of defects that any attempts to reduce will add more to cost than to value. It was assumed that workers cause defects, and inspections are necessary to insure quality. The outcome of this view is an emphasis on low costs and purchasing from low-cost suppliers through competitive bidding.

The current view is that quality lowers costs. Shank and Govindarajan (1993) quoted Deming as saying that 85 percent of quality problems are attributable to faulty systems and only 15 percent to labor. The reasons for faulty systems are difficult design, inferior inputs, inadequate maintenance, and poor working conditions. In other words, quality is a management problem. Solving these problems reduces the costs of inspection, rework and other quality related costs.

## TOTAL QUALITY MANAGEMENT STRATEGY

A total quality management strategy should be linked to the strategic vision of the business. It should link any quality initiative to customers, competitiveness and profitability. The level of customer satisfaction defines quality. A quality process should identify and quantify the costs of poor quality. Performance rewards should be based on quality and customer satisfaction measures.

## TOTAL QUALITY MANAGEMENT PROCESSES

The first step is to create a measurement scheme that includes both direct measures of quality and measures of cost of quality. The four categories of cost of quality—prevention, appraisal, internal failure and external failure—are discussed in Key 8. The direct measures of quality include measures of all facets of a firm's activities. Examples are: machine up-time, rate of output, adherence to production and delivery schedules, and the percentage of output that is first quality. The direct measures of quality: can be easily quantified and understood by factory employees. These measures provide useful information because they direct attention to a process that needs correction. An emphasis on quality typically leads to process improvements and increased efficiency. It is difficult to produce a quality product with a poorly conceived process.

## IDENTIFYING QUALITY PROBLEMS

Managers use control charts, cause-and-effect

analysis, and Pareto Charts (see below) to identify quality problems. These tools provide information signals to identify quality problems. Warning signals tell the manager that a problem needs to be investigated. Diagnostic signals identify the problem and provide information on how to correct it.

## CONTROL CHARTS

◆ Display variations in a process and help to analyze the variations over time.

◆ Distinguish between random variations and variations that should be investigated.

◆ Provide a warning signal when variations are beyond a specified level.

## CAUSE-AND-EFFECT ANALYSIS

Cause-and-effect analysis provides diagnostic signals that identify potential causes of defects using a two-step approach. It defines the defect and defines events that contribute to the defect (e.g., human factors, methods and design, machine-related factors, and materials and components factors).

## PARETO CHARTS

Pareto Charts are a set of bar graphs that display the number of defects over time. Pareto Charts help identify the defects that have the highest occurrence and help set priorities of quality improvement efforts.

# KEY 23

## Performance measures in multi-unit organizations

In large organizations, the delegation of decision-making authority is common. The benefits of decentralization are: local information can mean better decisions at local levels, free up central management from operational decision making and reduce information overload. Unit managers may make decisions that benefit themselves instead of maximizing the value of the firm. Hence, there is a need for a performance measurement system that motivates unit managers to act in the interest of the whole company.

Such performance measurement systems depend on the type of unit. There are four types of decentralized units: cost centers where a manager only has control over costs (e.g., a plant); revenue centers where managers are responsible for generating sales, but may not be able to control product mix or costs; profit centers where managers have authority to determine product mix, set prices, and monitor production activities to control costs; investment centers where managers have control over costs, revenues, and the investment in assets.

The following table lists some of the performance measures that can be used in each type of center.

| Center | Performance measures |
|---|---|
| Cost center | Manufacturing costs |
| | Defect rates |
| | % of on time delivery |
| Revenue center | Sales volume in units |
| | Inventory turnover |
| | Sales revenue |
| Profit center | Manufacturing costs |
| | Distribution costs |
| | Sales volume |
| | Profitability |
| Investment center | Return on investment |
| | Market share |
| | Success of new products |
| | Economic value added |

## PROFIT CENTERS

Profit centers are popular means of management control because profitability is a simple way to monitor the effectiveness of a business unit. Profit is a powerful motivator. A profit center manager has control over critical factors of business (e.g., sales price, sales volume, costs). There is a clear definition of business unit boundaries. There is a belief that profit center measurements will motivate a profit center manager to behave in the interest of the whole firm. This will require acceptance of the fairness of the measurement system by profit center managers. It requires that the system be consistent with other management systems (e.g., compensation system, capital-budgeting system and organizational structure).

It is expected that profit center managers will be motivated to perform better than they did before the structure was adopted.

For these benefits to occur, senior management must find solutions to transfer pricing problems, which are the prices charged by one subunit to another subunit within a decentralized firm. Separate evaluation criteria for profit centers and profit center managers may be necessary, including the need for efficient communication that explains clearly the goals of top management to center managers and informs senior management of the aspirations of center managers. Strategies should be developed to set the tone and direction for the whole organization.

Plans are necessary to coordinate the various functions and the actions of the different centers, especially in multidivisional and multinational firms. Profit should only be used as a responsibility measure when profit is the result of actions by the manager being evaluated.

## Pseudo-profit centers

Many firms convert cost centers that provide components and services to other units into pseudo-profit centers. This is done to encourage entrepreneurial practices and use profit as a motivator. Creating internal enterprises encourages flexibility and responsiveness and promotes a customer focus. Success depends on senior management managing corporate structure, fostering collaborative synergy, and providing center managers with information because ownership of information empowers action.

An example of a pseudo-profit center is Xerox's Logistics and Distribution Center (Tucker & Zivan, 1985). The Logistics and Distribution Center

(L&D) is responsible for managing the ordering, receiving, warehousing, and transportation of all parts and consumables inventories for Xerox's Business Systems Group. L&D was converted from a cost center into a pseudo-profit center through four steps.

◆ Establishing benchmarks for expenses, inventory turns and levels of service.
◆ Negotiating service levels.
◆ Biding for business of sister units.
◆ Vending for outsiders. The objectives of turning L&D into a pseudo-profit center are to: stimulate a profit center environment, motivate employees and motivate internal customers to determine their true service needs.

### INVESTMENT CENTERS

Investment centers expand decentralization of profit centers by delegating the control of the investment in the center to its manager. The managers of investment centers control revenue, costs and investment. Return on investment (R.O.I.) is the typical performance measure used in evaluating investment centers. R.O.I.= Net income/total assets. The R.O.I. has two measurement issues: 1) Identifying income generated by the center. 2) Identifying and determining the value of a center's assets.

### RESIDUAL INCOME (R.I.) AND ECONOMIC VALUE ADDED

A second measure of performance of investment centers is residual income.

R.I. = Income after tax − Total annual cost of capital

The concept of residual income has been expanded into an economic value added (E.V.A.) concept that measures the contribution of a business unit, a project or a product to shareholders value. E.V.A. can be used in strategy formulation as E.V.A. can be increased either by earning more profit without raising more capital or use less capital to earn the same income.

R.O.I. can cause dysfunctional behavior where a manager may reject an investment whose return exceeds the firm's cost of capital because it reduces the center's R.O.I.

Example: a center that has a 20 percent R.O.I. may reject a project that has a 15 percent R.O.I. even though the firm's R.O.I. is only 10 percent. Using R.I./E.V.A. avoids these dysfunctional behaviors and provides a link between performance and shareholder value. Both methods have considerable measurement problems.

### INTER-CENTER RELATIONS

Even though organizations are decentralized, there remain many interdependencies. It is in the best interest of the organization that all subunits cooperate. Transfer pricing is an important factor in inter-profit center relations. Another issue is sharing of information. Ownership of information empowers action. Managers of profit centers are more concerned with finding the information they need than with providing information requested by senior management.

# KEY 24

## Transfer pricing

This is the price that one division or segment of an organization charges another division or segment of an organization for a product or service. Transfer prices should satisfy five objectives:

- ◆ Optimum decisions for the whole company.
- ◆ High managerial effort.
- ◆ Accurate performance evaluation.
- ◆ Goal congruence.
- ◆ Preservation of divisional autonomy.
- ◆ Minimize taxes.

Primary goal of transfer pricing is to achieve optimal decisions at the organizational level.

### THREE METHODS FOR TRANSFER PRICING

- ◆ Market-based transfer prices: use publicly available prices. These are ideal for competitive intermediate market and independent subunits.
- ◆ Cost-based transfer prices: use actual or

standard costs. Used when intermediate market does not exist or market prices are too costly to obtain.

◆ Negotiated transfer prices: use mutually agreed prices.

## GENERAL RULE FOR TRANSFER PRICING

$$\begin{matrix} \text{Minimum} \\ \text{Transfer} \\ \text{Price} \end{matrix} = \begin{matrix} \text{Additional outlay costs} \\ \text{per unit incurred to} \\ \text{transfer point} \end{matrix} + \begin{matrix} \text{Opportunity costs} \\ \text{per unit to the} \\ \text{selling division} \end{matrix}$$

Example: Division X makes switches that can be sold either to Division Y or external customers. Operating data on the 2 divisions are:

| Division X: | |
|---|---|
| Unit selling price to outside | $30 |
| Variable product cost | $16 |
| Variable S&A cost | $4 |
| Fixed production costs | $500,000 (for 100,000 units) |
| Division Y: | |
| Outside purchase price $30 (before volume discount) | |

Division Y now purchases the switches from outside at $30 less a 10 percent volume discount. Since quality is the same for outside supplier and Division X, Division Y is considering internal transfer.

The controller of X has determined that half of the variable S&A can be avoided on an intracompany sale. Top management wants to treat each division as autonomous with independent profit responsibility.

Assume that Division X is selling 60,000 units per year to outside customers and Division Y needs 40,000 units per year.

◆ What is the lowest transfer price justifiable?

- What is the highest transfer price justifiable?
- If Division Y finds a supplier charging $26 per unit, should Division X be required to meet this price?

Solutions:

- Transfer price = Variable costs + Opportunity cost = $18 + $0**
  $16 + ($4 × 50 percent) = $18

** Opportunity cost is zero because division X has enough idle capacity to meet Division Y demand.

- Highest transfer price = Market price − Volume discount = ($30 − $3) = $27
- No, Division X must be free to reject intracompany business to pursue more profitable business. However, Division X will be foolish to turn down Division Y's offer because it has idle capacity.

# KEY 25

## *Balanced scorecard*

---

The balanced scorecard is a set of performance targets and results measures that stresses meeting an organization's objectives and its responsibilities to various stakeholders. It helps an organization to systematically develop a comprehensive and internally consistent planning and control system. Four key performance criteria are used in the balanced scorecard: financial, customer satisfaction, innovation and learning, and internal business processes.

In an environment of heightened competition and change, performance measures have become a critical managerial tool—"What gets measured gets done." Firms need performance measures that focus on their missions and strategies. The current focus on financial measures has been criticized because:

- ◆ Financial measures are reported too late and focus on the short-term.
- ◆ Current financial measures do not capture

important sources of value creation such as intellectual capital.

◆ Financial measures are not customer driven.
◆ Short-term emphasis on financial measures can lead firms to focus on quick fixes and ignore the need to create long-term value.
◆ When firms used nonfinancial measures, they are used independent of financial measures.

### THE BALANCED SCORECARD

Kaplan and Norton (1993) developed the balance scorecard to address the criticism. It is a comprehensive framework that translates strategic objectives into a coherent set of performance measures of four criteria: financial, customer satisfaction, innovation and learning, and internal processes. The specific measures should answer the following questions:

◆ Financial: How do we look to our shareholders?
◆ Customer satisfaction: How do we look to our customers?
◆ Innovation and learning: Are we able to sustain innovation, change and improvement?
◆ Internal processes: What business processes are the value drivers?

Its structure integrates the four criteria. For example, to increase return on capital we may need to improve the customer satisfaction measure on time delivery, which depends on improving quality and cycle time, which depend on employee learning.

Such integration enables a firm to see when an action in one area may have a negative impact on another area. For example, a firm may decide to increase quarterly revenues by changing production schedules to move ahead jobs with a shorter process cycle time. This may decrease on-time delivery and affect customer satisfaction. Without the balanced scorecard, a firm may not notice such an impact.

Another feature of the balanced scorecard is that it points the lead and lag relationships between the four criteria. Improving internal processes and employee skills are leading indicators that are necessary for the lagging indicator customer satisfaction, which precede the financial indicators.

#### CHARACTERISTICS OF BALANCED SCORECARD
- Keep it simple: a balanced scorecard with 4 to 10 measures.
- Mix outcome measures and performance indicators.
- Choose the appropriate benchmark — internal or external.
- Show relationship between department and core process. Never let department measures become more important than process measures.

#### EXAMPLE OF THE BALANCED SCORECARD MEASURES
Financial measures:
- Return on capital employed.
- Cash flow.
- Project profitability.
- Sales backlog.
- Economic value added.
- Market value added.

Customer measures:
- Customer satisfaction index.
- Market share.
- Customer retention.

- ◆ New customer acquisition.
- ◆ Customer profitability.
- ◆ On-time delivery.

## INNOVATION AND LEARNING

- ◆ Proportion of revenue from new products.
- ◆ Employee training.
- ◆ Employee retention.
- ◆ Employee skills level.
- ◆ Information technology process.
- ◆ Internal business processes.
- ◆ First quality, first time.
- ◆ Cycle time.
- ◆ Cost reduction.
- ◆ Scrap.
- ◆ Rework.
- ◆ Returns.

## REFERENCES

Cooper, R., Kamakura Ironworks Company Ltd., Harvard Business School Case 9-195-056, 1994.

Cooper, R., Citizen Watch Company Ltd., Harvard Business School Case 9-194-033, 1994.

Cooper, R., and R. S. Kaplan, "Profit Priorities from Activity-Based Costing," *Harvard Business Review*, May-June 1991, pp. 130–135.

Cooper, R., and R. S. Kaplan, *The Design of Cost Management Systems*, 2nd ed., Prentice Hall, 1998.

Dyer, J. H., "How Chrysler Created an American Keiretsu," *Harvard Business Review*, July–August 1996, pp. 2–11.

Kaplan, R. S., Kanthal (A) & (B), Harvard Business School Cases 9-195-056, 1994.

Kaplan, R. S. and D. P. Norton, "The Balance Scorecard: Measures that Drive Performance," *Harvard Business Review*, January–February 1992, pp. 71–79.

Kaplan, R. S. and Atkinson, *Advanced Management Accounting*, 3rd ed., Prentice Hall, 1998.

Maher, M. W., *Cost Accounting: Creating Value for Management*, 5th ed., Irwin, 1997.

Porter, M. E., *Competitive Advantage*, The Free Press, 1985.

Shank, J. and V. Govindarajan, *Strategic Cost Management*, Free Press, 1993.

Simon, R., Codman & Shertleff Inc.: Planning and Control System, Harvard Business School Case 9-187-081, 1987.

Simon, R., "Control in the Age of Empowerment," *Harvard Business Review*, March-April 1995, pp. 80–88.

Spardlin, R. C. C. Konstans, and Kasischke, "Controlling Cash Constrained Enterprises," *Managerial Planning*, July-August 1976, pp. 36–40.

Tucker, F. G. and S. M. Zivan, "A Xerox Cost Center Imitates a Profit Center," *Harvard Business Review*, May–June 1995, pp. 2–4.

# INDEX

## AUTHOR

**MOHAMED HUSSEIN**, Ph.D., has taught in the University of Connecticut's undergraduate, MBA, EMBA, and doctoral programs. He has served as resident director of UConn's Program in European Studies at the University of Maastricht, The Netherlands, and was the Andersen Consulting Faculty Fellow at UConn. He has written books on accounting and control systems for small business and on starting a small business in the state of Connecticut. Dr. Hussein's research has been published in journals such as *Accounting, Organizations and Society, Auditing: A Journal of Practice & Theory*, and the *International Journal of Accounting.*